MOTORCYCLING
The Golden Years

MOTOR CYCLING
The Golden Years

A PICTORIAL ANTHOLOGY
COMPILED BY
RUPERT PRIOR

TIGER BOOKS INTERNATIONAL
LONDON

CLB 4047
This edition published 1994 by
Tiger Books International PLC, London
© 1994 CLB Publishing, Godalming, Surrey
All rights reserved
Printed and bound in Italy
ISBN 1 85501 342 8

CONTENTS

"Rocket" and Motorcycles – Pioneers of the Motorcycle –
Motor Cycling at the Beginning – The Era of the Motor
Bicycle from 1900 to 1904 – Charles Jarrot's Motor Cycle
Races – The 1904 International Cup Race – An American
Head Protector – Round the Track – The Motor Cycle and
its Development – Diana Awheel.

The Great Race 1911 – An American Victory – The One
and Only... 1921 BMCRC 500 Mile Race at Brooklands –
New Italian Track – Nuvolari – Racing Through the
Century – Hubert Hassall on Continental Events – W.D.
Marchant. The Famous Speedman – The Nürberg Ring
Opened – Racing Fever – Grand Prix d'Europe-Rome 1932
– The Value of Good Pitwork.

Motorcycling, Motoring and Flying – Guthrie, the Racing
"Star" – Motor Cycle Racing – 100 Miles in the Hour –
Brooklands or Montlhéry – Record Breaking in the Dark –
Ernst Henne, the World's Speediest Motorcyclist – Henne
does it again – Records Course – Records Abroad –
180mph on a Five-Hundred! – Fernihough does it again! –
Motor Cycle Racing-Prospects for 1937 – Streamlining has
come to stay! – 170mph-on Two Wheels – Racing Breeds
Car Champions.

MOTOR CYCLES
by F. Straight
Secretary of the Auto Cycle Club

There are many aspiring motorists to whom the original cost of a motor car, and its upkeep when purchased, is a barrier to ownership. Hence the favour with which motor cycles are regarded and the importance they have attained in the automobile movement. This is not to be wondered at when one considers the comparatively low cost, the very little that is required for the upkeep of a motor cycle, either of the two- or three-wheel variety, and, particularly in the case of the motor bicycle, the very little storage accommodation that is required.

There is no doubt that the motor cycle will prove an effective educational medium in connection with automobilism, for the intending motorist is able to learn all about petrol engines at a much less cost than is demanded by the purchase of a motor-car. The experience thus gained is extremely useful should the motor cyclist ultimately become the owner of a larger vehicle, and those who begin with motor cycles invariably enter the ranks of motor-car owners after they have realised the pleasures and delights of automobilism, whether with the cheaper or more expensive form. For some reason or other the idea has got abroad that motor cycling is a pastime that will not long survive, but the fact that up to the end of June 1905 the number of motor cycles registered in the United Kingdom was 34,700 shows how popular it has become. Those who have once tasted the pleasures of roaming through the country on a motor cycle, either of the two- or three-wheeled type, only give it up to go in for a car, and this because of the more sociability and the better luggage carrying facilities of the latter. On the other hand one frequently hears of men who after an experience of cars, revert again to the motor cycle on account of the pleasure and independence in being without a mécanicien.

The possession of a licence to drive a motor car entitles the holder to drive a motor cycle, but a licence to drive a motor-cycle does not give authority to drive a motor car. Restive horses and policemen must be respected, and the motor cyclist must halt upon a signal from the driver of the former or the raising of the hand of the latter. Lights must be carried as on ordinary bicycles. Efficient brakes must also be provided.

Apart from machines now regarded as curiosities, the motor tricycle of MM. de Dion and Bouton was the most successful form of vehicle introduced after the adaptation of the internal combustion engine to road locomotion. The first made had a small 3/4 hp. motor fixed to the rear axle, the carburetter being placed behind the main down tube to the frame. The size of the motor was gradually increased. The Beeston tricycle was the first of the kind English-made throughout, but the Ariel motor-tricycle was the first really successful English machine. It showed several variations in design from the original De Dion. Notably, the motor, instead of being placed to the rear of the back axle was placed forward of it. Altogether the tricycle is a type of machine which has been very much neglected in its single form. It is difficult to understand why, unless it is, that being a three-wheeler it requires more storage accommodation than a motor-bicycle; on the other hand, it has certain advantages, particularly in the matter of side-slip.

Of late years there has sprung up a demand for some sort of attachment by which the rider can take a passenger out with him, and various forms of attachments have been placed upon the market, viz., fore-carriages, side-carriages, and trailers. The fore-carriage, or 'trimo' as it was frequently called, the basket or body of which was detachable, so that the machine could be ridden as a tricycle or, by detaching one wheel, be converted into a motor-bicycle, bid fair to become popular, but this has now given place to the more powerful tri-car, which has arrived at such a state of perfection that it is really a small car. This type of machine is fitted in most cases with a

Wealthy boulevardier: Count Albert De Dion, as seen by *Vanity Fair*, astride a De Dion tricycle. If the new-born motorcycle industry was to succeed it needed a reliable source of petrol engines. Gottleib Daimler, arguably the first to make a petrol-driven motorcycle, in 1885, had involuntarily shown the way for rival engineers and the ambitious Count studied the Daimler pattern closely. De Dion enlisted two penurious model makers, Bouton and Trépardoux, and produced a petrol engine for sale as a proprietary or 'loose' power unit. Orders poured in and other makers developed their own brands of proprietary engines, many inspired by De Dion-Bouton's enterprise.

The Belgian firm Minerva made motorcycles from 1910 to 1914 (and motor cars from 1905 to 1939). Minerva supplied engines from 2hp to 8hp to other producers, and manufacturing licences to other countries.

The mechanisms of the early motorcycle were very close to the road and entirely exposed to rain, mud and grit. *Engineering* reported: one had to be either a 'very enthusiastic mechanical amateur, or a devoted seeker after notoriety'. In the opinion of another contemporary, 'the attempt to attach motors to bicycles is a mistake'.

twin-cylinder engine of from 6 to 10 h.-p., with water cooling, the circulation being made positive by centrifugal pump, geared direct from the engine-shaft. The objection to a side-carriage is the difficulty of riding the machine when there is only the driver, the general practice being to sit in the side carriage and steer the machine, which it must be admitted, is not very comfortable, although Messrs. Mills and Fulford claim that in their "Castor Wheel" side-car they have overcome the difficulty. Trailers have lost their popularity, and this is not to be wondered at for there is always the fear of the bicycle having a side-slip, which of course would mean trouble for the occupant of the trailer.

Although Daimler designed a motor bicycle in 1885, it was not till eight or nine years ago that serious and sustained efforts were made to perfect the petrol motor bicycle. In this connection the Wulfmuller was a pioneer. It had a double-cylinder motor, driving the hind wheel, and was a cumbersome and unsuccessful machine.

The Werner occupied for some years a similar position among motor bicycles to the De Dion among motor tricycles, but within the last two or three years English manufacturers have come rapidly to the front; in fact, sixteen out of the twenty one motor cycles which succeeded in obtaining awards in the Auto-Cycle Club's six days Reliability Trials in 1905, were of English manufacture throughout including the engines. It speaks well for the reliability of the present motor cycle that twenty-one machines should have passed successfully such a series of trials without being attended to in any way beyond having daily supplies of petrol and lubricating oil. Most motor bicycles have been adapted for belt driving. A few, however, are driven by chains, and in the 4 cylinder F.N. we have a bevel-gear-driven single-track machine. The engine is placed in a vertical position in front of the crank bracket, and the drive is then taken through a pair of spur wheels. These are cut at a slight angle, the power is then transmitted down a propeller shaft which is enclosed in the bottom stay of the bicycle frame, terminating with a small bevel pinion which meshes on a larger bevel fixed on the hub of the driving wheel, all the running parts being mounted on ball bearings.

The position of the engine was one of the early difficulties manufacturers of motor cycles had to contend with, and in the early Werner machines the motor was fixed above the front wheel. It was long thought that the weight of the engine should be placed as high upon the bicycle as possible. That location, it was claimed, was necessary to ensure the stability of the machine, and to minimise the danger of side-slip. Experience, however, has shown that this is not so essential, and in the majority of cases the engine is placed halfway between the two wheels in a vertical position, thus bringing the centre of gravity very low. A low-down position between the wheels is being generally adopted, as tending to reduce the vibration and lessen the liability to side-slip.

The subject of side-slip is one of the greatest interest to all motor cyclists, and the position of the motor has been variously located, with a view of minimising its occurrence. It is generally acknowledged that motor bicycles are not more prone to dangerous side slips than are ordinary leg-propelled cycles. On a slippery road with the ordinary bicycle there is only the rider and the bicycle in question, but in the case of the motor bicycle the engine makes its presence felt, lessening that instantaneous and automatic control so essential for safety.

The frame is now generally built low and 26-inch wheels fitted, thus bringing the rider nearer the ground, and enabling him to put out his foot when the machine is brought to a standstill, making a very much more comfortable machine, and considerably reducing the risk of side-slip.

The year 1905 saw a great increase in the horse-power of engines fitted, and most machines have now an engine of about $3^1/2$ hp., although in many cases engines of 4, 5, and 6 hp. are fitted, the latter being generally

twin-cylinder. The success of the twin-cylinder in the International Cup Race for auto-cycles which took place in France in June 1905, when Vondrick the Austrian rider averaged 53 miles per hour over a distance of 170 miles, has no doubt increased the popularity of the multi-cylinder engine, a large number of twin-cylinder engines being fitted to English made motor-cycles, whilst some of the foreign machines, notably the F.N. and the Durkopp, have four-cylinder engines. It is very satisfactory to find that some of the names so well-known in connection with the manufacture of cycles are amongst the leading firms of motor cycle manufacturers; in addition to the Triumph Cycle Co. and Singer & Co., the Quadrant Cycle Company of Birmingham have attained a very high reputation for their motor bicycles, which are fitted with a $3^1/2$hp. engine, and their Quadrant Carette is looked upon as one of the leading makes of tri-car. The Ariel Co., one of the pioneers of the British built throughout motor cycle, is another firm who maintain their standard of excellence in the motor bicycles which they have placed upon the market.

The extensive employment of the Minerva motor was one of the most astonishing features of the early development in motor bicycles. It is noteworthy, however, that several makers, whilst still using Minerva engines, have introduced in connection with it a number of special features which considerably facilitates the handling of the machine.

Power transmission, a subject already incidentally mentioned, is an important point with regard to motor bicycles.

Belt-driving was originally the only medium considered, as it overcomes much of the vibration, although the tendency of the belt to slip is an obvious disadvantage. The V section belt is the type most generally used, and is made either of leather, rubber or canvas.

In the Singer motor bicycle the manufacturers have departed from their custom of locating the whole of the mechanism in the driving wheel, and the 3

hp. engine is carried vertically in a frame of special construction. A spray type of carburetter and magneto ignition are employed, and the control is by means of the usual levers fitted on the top tube. These machines are fitted with belt transmission. Chain transmission is employed in the Phelon and Moore motor bicycle, a friction disc faced with leather being introduced to slip

Rochet poster, 1907
The Parisian Rochet was one of the first companies to produce motorcycles with two-speed gearboxes. The company existed until 1910.

In 1902 the designer George Gibson wrote: 'It is a most curious comment on our engineering ability to see motors strapped in all sorts of funny positions to a bicycle frame'.

slightly when undue pressure falls on the chain. In this case the motor is an essential part of the frame, and forms the bottom tube. The machines are very similar to those manufactured by the well-known firm of Humber & Co. of Coventry, who have, however, now given up the manufacture of motor bicycles.

Personally the writer is in favour of chain transmission. During the very wet season of 1903 he rode a Humber, and throughout never had any trouble whatever with the chains, although the machine was ridden in all kinds of weather.

Future developments in connection with motor bicycles will no doubt be concerned with spring frames and two-speed gears. Already some interesting work in these

directions has been done, and in the Bat spring frame bicycle we have a machine that is not only comfortable but which reduces vibration to a minimum. This machine went successfully through the Auto-Cycle Club's 1,000 Mile Reliability Trial in the worst possible weather, securing a first-class certificate. The Triumph and Quadrant machines both have spring front forks which are very effective, and add considerably to the comfort of the rider.

One drawback to the use of the motor bicycle in hilly districts is that the motor only gives out its full power when running at the normal speed. When going uphill the speed of the motor naturally slackens, and consequently the engine does not give off its standard capacity. To overcome this difficulty inventors are studying the matter from two different points of view. Some are in favour of the use of motors of higher capacity than those now in general use, while others are experimenting with two-speed gears, arguing that it is better to have a small engine kept steadily running, and so developing its full power notwithstanding the gradient, the low gear being used for hill climbing. The Phoenix motor bicycles are fitted with two-speed gears, and, indeed, many of the leading manufacturers fit them if desired. The Phoenix two-speed gear is contained in the back hub, and the power from the engine to the two-speed gear is transmitted through a friction clutch. A lever placed on the top tube of the machine when pulled right back engages the high gear, when placed vertically gives a free engine, enabling it to be started with a handle like a car, and when pushed further forward the low gear gradually engages by means of a friction clutch, so that the machine can be started even on an incline. The gear being in the back wheel only travels at the same speed as that wheel;

therefore, going very slowly, it is practically noiseless. It is disappointing that change-speed gears have not made greater progress, for there is no doubt that it is in this direction that improvement is needed, and with a fool-proof change speed gear we shall be nearer the perfect motor bicycle.

Motor cycling should prove attractive to ladies of a mechanical turn of mind, and already machines have been specially introduced for their benefit. The motor is placed below the bottom tube, and ample protection is afforded in the way of dress-guards, etc.

Before setting out, the cycle should be carefully examined and the engine tried. It is necessary, too, to be assured that the tool-bag contains the requisite equipment of tools and spare parts.

The owner of a motor cycle who expects to use it constantly without previous experience, and not run up against various sources of stoppage and breakage, will find himself mistaken. A frequent experience is to run the whole gamut of troubles, and thus by actual knowledge having learned to fix all the various parts, the operator is qualified to take care of his machine. These troubles occur for three principal reasons. First, the ordinary individual who buys a motor cycle will not make a careful study of the manner in which the machine is built and how it works, but prefers to tackle it on the "hit and miss" plan and learn by hard knocks and experience. Second, carelessness and the disinclination many persons have to take proper care of a piece of machinery. A motor cycle, however, cannot be expected to run properly unless it receives regular attention. Third, from accidents pure and simple. As already explained, a great deal of trouble might be avoided if riders would only take the pains to understand the principle of the machine before attempting long journeys.

Advertising from Marchal. Primitive forms of lighting by oil and acetylene came into use from the mid-1890s. Early motorcycles, in appearance resembling an ordinary, although rather heavily made, push bike, were inherently unstable, suffered from appalling vibration and a vunerability to the elements. Night riding called for considerable skill and self-confidence.

Boasting the 'largest factory in the world', Clément were among a number
of French manufacturers offering 'loose' engines to a burgeoning
motorcycle industry.

FROM PEDALS TO PETROL

"The novice need have no fear of his motor bicycle. It is not a haphazard aggregation of bits of metal, and although there are bicycle motors composed of more then 140 separate pieces, they present no unfathomable mystery."

F. Straight, Secretary of the Auto Cycle Club

"ROCKET" AND MOTORCYCLES
The World on Wheels H.O. Duncan

In this country new inventions have always been more or less ridiculed. When the first steam engine, the "Rocket," was built by Stephenson and put to run on rails, he was ridiculed all over the country. Stephenson, however, sat down to the ridicule and it did not harm him at all. What was the result? The world was now covered with a network of railways. Then there came the introduction of the ordinary bicycle and that suffered the same fate, so far as ridicule was concerned, as the railways.

The first riders of bicycles were met with ridicule. What is seen today? Why, all the world on two wheels.

Two years ago the same ridicule was poured upon motorcycling. People are now beginning to turn around and see that the introducers of the motorcycle were not such fools as they were put down to be.

PIONEERS OF THE MOTOR-CYCLE

If the motor industry offers so many striking examples of energy, enterprise and initiative, there is surely no branch in which these qualities have shown up more conspicuously than in the development of the motorcycle trade. The motorcycle owes its birth to two Russians, Michel and Eugène Werner, whose initiative and perseverance created a vogue for the little machine by which hundreds of cycle firms are now profiting.

Michel and Eugene Werner were for some years engaged in journalistic work in Moscow, where they founded and carried on different publications. But the repressive newspaper laws of that country decided these enterprising brothers to settle down in France in the hope of finding a better outlet for their talents. Taking up alternately typewriting machines, phonographs and cinematographs, they sought to introduce improvements into each. This somewhat over-crowded field,

however, did not seem to offer them many opportunities, and it was not until the motor-car began to attract attention that the brothers hit upon their true vocation.

The motor-car was still regarded as a crude and experimental vehicle when the brothers Werner saw that there was a vast opening for business if only they could propel bicycles by motive power. The car was the luxury of a few.

Why should they not produce a light, portable form of vehicle, which should come within the reach of everybody by simply fitting a small motor to an ordinary type of bicycle?

Some such attempts had already been made with the Hildebrand and Wolfmüller, the Dalifol steam bicycle, the Millet petrol bicycle with five cylinders set in the back wheel, and one or two others. But the Werner Brothers were the first to approach the matter in a thoroughly practical manner, with the aid of the little high-speed petrol motors then making their appearance on the market.

In 1896 they built a motor-bicycle with a single cylinder horizontal motor in the rear with transmission to the driving wheel by chain and a friction disk. The results were not encouraging. Then the idea occurred to them of fixing the motor to the head tube and employing a belt to transmit the power from the pulley on the countershaft to the front wheel. The principle appeared so simple and effective that its application was patented. In 1897, the brothers started to manufacture their "motorcyclette" and turned out 12 in the course of the year.

Although the Werner machine was the object of much curiosity, the practical results were not all that could be desired. As electrical ignition was not sufficiently perfected to allow of its use on these little high-speed motors, the machines had to be fitted with tube ignition. This was neither convenient nor comfortable, especially in the hot summer months when the hot air from the burner perpetually "fanned" the rider's nose! The appearance of the few

Posing for the camera: enthusiast E. Cook with 1901 F.D. Werner.
Among the fortune hunters from Paris attempting to exploit the enormous opportunities thrust upon a new industry by an ever-increasing public demand were the Werner brothers, probably the greatest pioneers in motor-cycling. When, in 1901, they decided to improve their power-bicycles and their reputation by going road-racing, they ably dominated the international races with victories for Rivièrre, their chief engineer, and Werner-fancier Auguste Bucquet. Vital improvements followed: reinforced forks, better electrics and a new spray carburettor. More race wins encouraged the Werner *Frères* to market what was surely the world's first racing replica, the 'Paris-Vienna Sport.'

devotees of machines – soiled with oil and their faces perspiring with heat – was not likely to predispose the public in favour of the motor-bicycle. Our experience with one of the first machines showed it to be entirely practical and a satisfactory "runner", but its one serious defect was smothering the rider with oil thrown up by the fly-wheel. The first experimental trip ruined our clothes. This "oil bath" was avoided by fitting dust-proof bushes to hold the oil.

The reluctance of the public to go in for motorcycling seemed anything but an encouraging outlook for the Messrs. Werner; but, fortunately, unhoped for support with English capital entirely changed the aspect of affairs. The Motor Manufacturing Company Ltd. – at that time on the lookout for something practical to manufacture – saw great possibilities in the Werner motor-bicycle. Negotiations were entered into for the purchase of the patents.

One of the directors of the company –

Laurin and Klement, Type CCCC. Laurin and Klement was a purely Bohemian enterprise founded in what was then the Austro-Hungarian Empire by a former bookseller (Vaclav Klement) and a skilled mechanic (Vaclav Laurin). 'The Mercedes among motorcycles' was their slogan and thanks to the competitive instincts of their backer, Count Alexander Kolowrat, the Prague firm earned a first-class sporting reputation. Laurin and Klement amalgamated with R.A.F. in 1913 and when Bohemia became part of the independent state of Czechoslovakia they were taken over by Karl Loevenstein's armaments company – Skodovy Zavody – and the new proprietors turned their enthusiasm to cars under the trademark Skoda.

Mr. Robinson – went to Paris to see the machine. Having ridden an ordinary bicycle, he decided to test it himself in the Bois de Boulogne. After a comfortable spin around the lake, he admitted more gas with the idea of trying the machine for speed. It was not long before the spectators saw the bicycle swerving from side to side and the rider making desperate attempts to keep it straight. Suddenly there was a mixture of a man and a motor-bicycle in a cloud of dust, then flame and smoke. Rider and machine had parted company, Mr Robinson rising in the air and falling heavily while the bicycle skidded along the road. The lamp to heat the platinum tube had set fire to the petrol and the machine was now a mass of flames.

Mr. Robinson, in attempting to break his fall, had badly cut his hands with what old cyclists know as the "gravel rash"; conveyed to a chemists, where it was found that he was not seriously hurt, his hands and elbows were dressed with bandages. The motor-bicycle was quickly dragged from the spilt petrol and the flames put out with some sand from the road.

After this experience, Michel Werner felt that his hopes had "vanished in smoke". Had this been so, the history of the motorcycle might have been a little different. But Mr. Robinson was fully aware that the accident had been due to his own inexpert handling of the machine and that, with proper management, the Werner bicycle would prove satisfactory. The brothers Werner were agreeably surprised to receive an invitation to visit London and conclude negotiations.

Messrs. Werner, with the money they received, were able to lay down new works and turn out their motor-bicycles on a commercial scale. In 1898 they build 300 machines and 500 in the following year; but still the demand hung fire, apparently because the public was not favourably dis-

posed towards the fitting of the motor on the steering-head tube. Thus for three years the inventors worked hard, with only indifferent success, to create a movement towards motorcycling.

The placing of the motor upon a bicycle was a most difficult problem at the time. All kinds of positions were adopted by various makers and none seemed to "hit the mark". However, in 1900 Michel Werner had a sudden inspiration – why not put the motor in place of the crank bracket? It was another "happy thought". So the Werner Brothers placed their 1¾ h.p. motor vertically at the bottom of the frame, at an equal distance between the front and back wheels. Being near the ground, the centre of gravity was lower than that of the majority of motorcycles on the market, and the tendency to side-slip was greatly lessened. This system was patented and the design registered. It proved to be just what the public wanted.

MOTOR CYCLING AT THE BEGINNING
by Charles Jarrot

I do not think motor bicycles ever appealed to me until, in the spring of 1897, I was strolling through the Bois de Boulogne one morning when I saw Fournier come flying along the road mounted on a motorcycle.

The machine was of an extraordinary length – almost as long as one of the ordinary triplets used for pacing purposes; a little motor was carried out near the back wheel – which extended some four or five feet behind the rider – and it was fitted with a pedalling gear of huge dimensions. The whole appearance of the machine was so racy that I did not rest until I had bought it.

I saw another motor bicycle about two days afterwards, which I also bought. This machine was one made throughout by Messrs. De Dion-Bouton, whereas Fournier's machine had been built by some enthusiastic cycle maker merely as a freak. The De Dion machine, however, was in the possession of Charron. He demonstrated its running capabil-

ities to me in his usual dashing style. It was a very neat machine, with the motor suspended between the frame, which was a shade longer than an ordinary bicycle, and was built of specially strong tubing.

The motor drove the back wheel of the bicycle by means of a flat leather band. One had to start it by running alongside, getting the gas and ignition rightly adjusted, then switching on the spark, and jumping into the saddle after the first two or three explosions. Of course, if you missed the saddle it was a serious matter, because, as happened to a friend of mine who attempted to ride the machine, it would then dash off by itself. I do not know that I ever cared very much for this little bicycle – it never seemed to go fast enough. It had to be geared fairly low for hill-climbing purposes, and also it was impossible to assist it by pedalling, as the pedals were fixed.

The other speed-instrument, however, which I had bought from Fournier was quite a different machine. In the first place, it required tremendous muscular effort to get it going at all. It was all built of very heavy tubing, and weighed some hundreds of pounds. The high pedalling gear – which was very useful when the machine was actually going – made it difficult to start from a standstill. One had to be very careful in switching on the motor, because, unless sufficient way was

Portrait of a great pioneer propagandist: Selwyn Francis Edge. Edge's racing career was short-lived (1899-1904), but he was a highly plausible company promoter, a worthy ambassador for the new-fledged industry and one of the generation of super-publicists who dominated the British motoring scene in the early years of the century.

obtained on the machine, the force of the explosion of the motor acting on the long connecting chains invariably broke them. I do not know how many new driving chains I fitted to that machine, until at last I had chains specially made of great strength.

The machine arrived in London one morning, and so keen was I to try it that I worked for two or three hours to get it into running order, and on that afternoon I started out for the country. I must have been plucky as well as foolish; many were the narrow escapes I had as I made my way out of London. I realised that if I once stopped it would be almost an impossibility for me to get going again, and I prayed that the traffic would not be so congested as to prevent my squeezing through.

Of course I created tremendous excitement, and I felt very proud of my new toy. Then, in an evil moment, an omnibus pulled in front of me and I had to jump off to save myself being thrown off. I walked some distance with the machine before I ventured to get on again, and then seeing a friendly lamp-post I thought this might afford me sufficient support in order to get into the saddle and start off again. I was fortunate enough to succeed in this, and, extraordinary to relate, I got through this ride without either breaking my neck or smashing up the machine.

After this, I had long rides, but never alone, only in the company of other motor cyclists who could be relied upon to give me assistance when it became necessary. To give an idea of the weight of the machine, I may say it was impossible for one man to lift it when it was lying on its side on the ground. Of course, so long as the machine could be kept going all was well, but directly it was allowed to slacken speed the motor gradually became more feeble and then stopped with a jerk, and I had to be very nimble in getting out of the saddle to prevent it falling on me. On one occasion I was reduced to such a state of exhaustion that when the machine stopped I simply fell off and the machine fell on top of me. There I lay, helpless and unable to move, not caring whether I proceeded further or remained where I was. Eventually my friends found me lying on the grass by the side of the road; four of us pushed the machine to the top of a hill, but it was a terrible effort.

The joy of that machine was tasted when it was really going well. The smoothness with which it travelled over the road in comparison with a motor tricycle was very marked, and the assistance one could give the motor by pedalling made a great difference to its speed. I was able to gauge what the delights of motor bicycling would be, provided the machine was fairly light, easily controlled, and reasonably powerful.

THE ERA OF THE MOTOR BICYCLE FROM 1900 TO 1904
By Eric W. Walford

It would be very difficult to say exactly why, at about this time, the motor bicycle revived in popularity and the "trike" waned in proportion. Makers had, of course, profited by their

Prévost (Alcyon), Circuit des Ardennes, Belgium 1905. The ancestor of all circuit racing, this race, dating from 1902, was the first event in which several laps of a closed circuit were covered. Known and represented in racing from pre-1914 days, the French Alcyon company won many races between the wars with their 173cc competition model ridden by Joly and Lemasson.

experience of the three wheeler and were finding out the faults of the motor bicycle, but it seems that the arrival of the belt drive, which Daimler had utilized so long ago, proved the turning point.

This belt drive, re-introduced by Werner, got rid, in one fell swoop, of all the troubles due to harsh transmissions, and though it introduced new troubles of its own, the greatest bogey – sideslip – was being laid. As an example of the change of feeling, one may quote perhaps an extract from a motor journal of the period which states that "... Although anticipated by the generality of people, there is, we think, little doubt that motor bicycles are likely to have a much greater vogue than is supposed".

The following extract from a letter by a well-known motor cyclist, Mr. Jo Pennell, the celebrated artist-author, describing a short tour in France on a front-drive Werner motor bicycle, may be of interest as giving a slight idea of what motorcycling was like in those days and what an experienced rider thought of it:

"But is a motor bicycle a practical touring machine? Excellent as it is for excursions, I am afraid not; ... but is the machine practical? Is it a rival to the ordinary cycle for touring? I think not .... The machine must be lubricated every 15 miles, and to have to stop to do so would be a bore ... while there are no means of carrying anything but a small amount of lubricant.

"But is the system right? I am afraid not for touring. I do not in this matter refer to the Werner especially, which seems to me to be the only motor bicycle at all practicable; all the others that I have seen have some fatal or absurd defect. But can a motor, of say 1 or 2

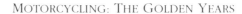

In competition: assorted makes under scrutiny for the Grand Prix de l'A.C.F. In the beginning France was the centre for motor sport. The first motorcycle race was the Paris-Nantes of 1896 and, in 1904, the first official international road race, the International Cup, was held at Dourdan.

horse-power, be attached to a bicycle? Can the bicycle be made strong enough to stand the strain ? And, if so, is it safe to ride, over all sorts of roads and under all sorts of conditions? I regret to say, I am afraid not ... But, if the strength is obtained, is it safe to ride at from 12-25 miles an hour uphill and downhill, on dry and wet roads, and through traffic? Though it is most fascinating, I believe it is equally dangerous."

When one considers that the motor cycle frame was little stronger than that of the ordinary "push" cycle, that the forks were exactly like "push" cycle forks, and not infrequently broke, that the tyres were very poor, and that sideslip was quite common, it is not surprising that it was somewhat of a toy. The makers must have considered it so, because they made no provision for lubrication of the engine from the seat, but expected one to stop every 10 or 20 miles and pour in oil from a can which one had to tie on anywhere as best one could. Really one had to be pretty hardened, or very enthusiastic, to be convinced that the motor bicycle was going to survive. The public looked upon it as a freak, whereas they had come to accept the "trike" as a practical proposition.

Nevertheless, by 1901, when motor bicycles were thought worthy of a lecture at the Society of Arts, small motorcycle manufacturers in Britain were buying foreign engines, such as the De Dion and Minerva, and building them into strengthened cycle frames. But although the larger manufacturers were beginning to market quite a number of machines they were to some extent handicapped by imports from the continent. These, however, helped to stimulate and improve the breed.

MY MOTOR CYCLE RACES
by Charles Jarrot

The end of May saw Edge and myself in Paris with the object of taking part in the motorcycle section of the Paris-Bordeaux race. We went over rather in the spirit of explorers. Our baggage was of a very meagre description, and we had but one idea – to see whether the sport of motor road-racing was all that had been claimed for it, and whether we could successfully play the game.

Our arrival at the Paris terminus began our troubles. We had seen our machines success-

23

fully lifted into the guard's van at Calais, and everything was arranged so simply that we imagined the preliminary difficulties were over. At Paris, however, we had to pass our machines through customs. I believe I had a maker's invoice which apparently saved me any further trouble, but in Edge's case he was not prepared with this. We explained to the custom officials that both machines were of identical construction, and that they were made by a French firm, and that we were merely bringing back into France what had originally come out of it. But the officials were obdurate.

Then Edge produced an extraordinary collection of articles. First he pulled out of his pocket a passport bearing an enormous red seal; this document the customs officials tried to seize, but Edge would not on any account let go of it. This had no effect except to infuriate the douaniers. He then produced a ticket of the Cyclists' Touring Club, a badge of the Cyclists' Touring Club, a badge of the Motor-Car Club, a membership ticket of the Automobile Club, and several other tickets and badges, pouring them in a heap on the table. Then, I think, the officials came to the conclusion that we were really people of great importance. Whether they imagined that these badges and tickets were some form of special decoration I do not know, but it all ended in Edge transferring his collection to his pocket and paying fifty centimes for a stamp which was stuck on to a big yellow document, which was duly signed by everybody present. We were then allowed to depart in peace.

The start took place from the bridge at Suresnes, and I was amazed to find such a number not only of spectators, but of competitors. The various cars were all ranged up in line – enormous 12 h.p. Panhards and various 10, 12 and 15 h.p. cars of other makes, all taking part in the race, the cars starting twenty minutes after the motor cyclists. There were seventy-eight entries altogether and, so dark was it at this hour, a considerable number set off with their lamps alight.

Our instructions at the start, so far as I could understand them, were exceedingly brief. An official with a red flag addressed the whole crowd of us lined up about four abreast – I think there were nine or ten rows all close up behind each other – and his speech was somewhat as follows:

"Gentlemen, this is Paris. There is Bordeaux" (pointing to the road). "There is but one thing you have to do – get there! Are you ready? Go!" Immediately, every rider put every ounce of energy into getting his machine started, and then the fun began. Some of the riders could not start at all, and were run into by the riders behind. Some managed to get a few explosions and then stopped, the riders frantically pedalling to keep the machines going. Others, attending to their taps and levers, instead of their steering, ran into the side of the road, and those of us who missed these many dangers fled away up the hill in a big bunch, enveloped in a great cloud of dust, hardly able to see an inch in front of us in the darkness, and trusting to luck to keep on the road at all.

Edge had started just in front of me, and within ten minutes I came upon him pushing his machine, evidently in trouble, but realising that it could not be serious I kept on my way. It seems that his engine "seized" immediately after the start.

And what a race we had! At that time, as no restrictions were made in regard to speed through the towns and villages, everybody rushed along having but one idea, namely to carry out the starter's instructions and get to Bordeaux. I was at that time in the best of physical condition, but the lack of sleep had affected me, and after two or three hours I began to feel tired; but there were many hours yet to go, and I realised that the ordeal was going to be very severe if I had any hope of reaching Bordeaux successfully. Then another horrible sensation overpowered me, and I began to be desperately hungry. This was a possibility which had never occurred to me. I had before starting put into my pocket some chocolate and some dried raisins, but when I came to hunt for these I

Sidecar in the Highlands of Scotland. The sidecar for long served as a means of providing a second or even a third seat, offering a reasonable degree of comfort, safety and weather protection. Wickerwork was popular for the first sidecars, followed by lightweight sprung frames with plywood or fabric covering. In later years steel and aluminium pressings were employed and were available in a variety of saloon and sporting styles.

Award-winning Sunbeam, 1913. A thoroughbred if ever there was one, Sunbeam turned from the manufacture of jappanned and tinplate products to motor engineering in 1899. Using simple, proven designs, with meticulous finish, the Wolverhampton factory were famous and successful racers, as evidenced in the twenties with the J.E. Greenwood-designed singles. The Model 90 has been called the finest example of British single-cylinder engineering.

THE PREMIER AWARD IN THE 1913 ENGLISH SIX DAYS A.C.U. REL
2¾ H.P. SUNBEAM. IT BEAT ALL OTHER MOTOR CYCLES IRRESPE

found that they had been reduced to a pulpy mass in my pocket, mixed up with the sand and dust which had been poured over me by the other racers.

To make matters worse the goggles with which I had provided myself were of a very primitive description. It was the first year that goggles had been considered necessary, and I found that those I had gave me very little protection. To add to our discomfort the cars which had started later began to overtake us. I forgot which of the cars came along first; I think it was Charron, but it took me little time to realise that he was travelling faster than I was, and as he came by I made a desperate effort and dropped in behind him, and there-

AM
YCLE
"Success"

ITY TRIALS WENT TO A
OF CLASS AND HORSE POWER.

terrifying, as I had no opportunity of seeing them before I struck them. It was all very thrilling while it lasted, and I stuck grimly on for miles and then my engine began to overheat, and to my despair I gradually dropped back. In the meantime, however, I had passed a number of motorcycles, and was in a very much better position than I had been before Charron's car assisted me. Then another car came along, but I found that another motor cyclist had followed my example, and was safely tucked in behind it. I made a desperate effort to hang on, but failed. On the next car coming by, however, I succeeded, and another 20 miles was covered in splendid style.

I was feeling terribly done, and my eyes were very painful from the dust. Then I arrived in a town which I was informed was Poitiers. Here I found a control where I had to sign my name in a book, and I was told that I was in third place and only a few minutes behind the leader, Bardin. I also obtained some refreshment, and started off again feeling much happier.

Within ten miles from Poitiers, however, the heavens seemed to open, and the rain came down in sheets. This was bad, but to my consternation my machine, which had previously run like clockwork, began to go very badly and my motor to misfire. It gradually became worse and worse, and then, with a sudden jerk, it stopped altogether. By this time I was reduced to a condition of absolute despair. Tired to death, aching all over, and my eyes causing me the most excruciating pain, I flung myself down in the road by my machine and there lay oblivious of everything.

I seemed to have lived a lifetime since the commencement of the race; Bordeaux appeared an impossible goal, and I seemed to have left Paris years before. My greatest trouble was in my eyes, and I tried to bathe them with my handkerchief soaked in rainwater. Shelter there was none. I seemed to have stopped in the middle of a wide, open, desolate plain. There was not even a shrub large enough to protect me from the down-

by obtained the benefit of his pacing, thus being drawn along behind the car with no wind resistance to overcome. It was a desperate game, as he, on a car fitted with springs, was able to take every inequality of the road, caniveaux, gutters, and pavé, at top speed, whereas I, on my little machine without springs of any sort, found these obstructions

Puch, Austria's oldest motorcycle factory, was established in 1903 and supplied numerous motorcycles to the army. In 1924, the lively Monza works racing two-stroke appeared. For 1929, the very fast water-cooled 248cc double-piston single, with a charging cylinder in the crankcase, was produced – victor of the 1931 German Grand Prix.

pouring rain, and I could conceive of no one being in a more unhappy plight.

One or two cars and one or two motor cyclists passed me, and then there was a big interval. Suddenly, a solitary rider appeared in the distance travelling very slowly. The figure appeared to be familiar, and presently, to my joy, I recognised it as Edge. Dismounting, he inquired what my trouble was, and in order to see whether my machine was really out of order he jumped on and pedalled it for ten or fifteen yards, but not an explosion could be obtained. He therefore rushed back to his mount saying that as he could not help me he would go on. Then he found that his own machine would not go either. We were therefore both stranded at the same spot in very much the same plight, both equally tired, both with machines which would not go, both wet through to the skin.

I should think we were delayed at this spot for an hour, and then it ceased raining, and we began wearily to push our way to the next village, which a kilometre stone advised us was some eleven kilometres away. The sun came out, the rain ceased, and then suddenly, without any warning, my machine started off again. I immediately sprang into the saddle and dashed off. Arriving in the village, I found a little auberge and discovered that they could give us some food. This I ordered, left my machine outside, and started to walk back along the road to render Edge assistance.

Then I saw a peculiar thing – a machine coming towards me and wandering from one side of the road to the other, apparently with no one controlling it. It certainly looked very uncanny, as I could not imagine where Edge had disappeared to and how the machine remained on the road. As I got nearer I discovered that Edge was pushing it, but he was so fatigued that he had laid his head down on the saddle, and, with both arms stretched out to the handle bars, was dragging himself along, pushing the machine in front of him, regardless of where it went; and in this position it was impossible to see his body from some distance away.

Our combined efforts enabled us eventually to arrive at the village, and after we had obtained some food we started off with renewed vigour on the rest of our journey – but we were not to arrive at Bordeaux that day. Edge broke a chain, and in trying to start his machine by running along and springing into the saddle over the back axle, he charged a curb, bending the axle and putting a wheel out of truth. I ran into a huge rocky boulder, which had been placed on the road by some miscreant for the benefit of the racing cars, and buckled my front wheel very badly. These delays, coupled with other troubles, made us resolve that we would spend the night at least in Angoulême and make Bordeaux on the following day, which we accordingly did.

Thus ended my first big motor cycle race. The experience I gained in it was invaluable, and I suppose its greatest charm lay in its novelty.

Bardin eventually won the race so far as the motorcycle section was concerned, and I found that he had accomplished his win in a very cunning manner. The reason our machine had stopped was because the rain, saturating the high-tension wire from the accumulator to the sparking plug, short-circuited the current. Bardin knew from experience that this happened, and as soon as it began to rain he, being near a farmhouse, dragged his machine under a shed, waited until the rain had ceased, and then went on his way without the running power of his machine having been affected in any way. It was another example of the old hand beating the novice.

INTERNATIONAL CUP RACE

The Motor Cycle Club of France organised the great International cup race in 1904 which was competed for by five nations – Austria, Denmark, France, Germany and Great Britain.

From half-past five in the morning, when it was barely daylight, thousands of motor cyclists and automobilists were congregated on and around the stands erected on each

side of the 14th milestone on the famous road between Dourdan and St. Arnoult, 40 miles from Paris.

Despite the early hour, we noticed several ladies, enveloped in warm furs, who had braved the cold to witness so important a contest. All the officials of the club were present, amongst whom we noticed Bardin (president) and Vital Bouhours (vice-president); Cormier, Deckert, and Bourcier de St. Chaffray. Tampier, the official timekeeper, gave the signal for the men to prepare to start just before six o'clock; the weather was magnificent, and the sun was doing its utmost to struggle through the clouds.

Around the starting-point the greatest enthusiasm prevailed, Demester being surrounded by a crowd of excited admirers. The machines of the British racing team were considerably admired, and they all possessed a fine turn of speed. T. Silver told us he thought the road was ideal for racing and he quite expected to average 50 miles per hour.

The men were now drawn up in line ready to start. One mishap alone accounted for a non-starter, in the person of Carl Muller (Berlin), whose Brennabor was burnt at dawn.

The road was lined all along with spectators, while numbers of motor cyclists who were showing off greatly interfered with the riders. At Dourdan, St. Arnoult and Ablis,

Man and Machine: a Brooklands Impression. Brooklands, in Surrey, the first proper motor course in the world, opened for business in 1907. The first known motorcycle event was a match race in 1908. Brooklands became a unique institution where racing was a happy alliance between the amateur and the professional and where the intense rivalry was tempered with friendship and fun.

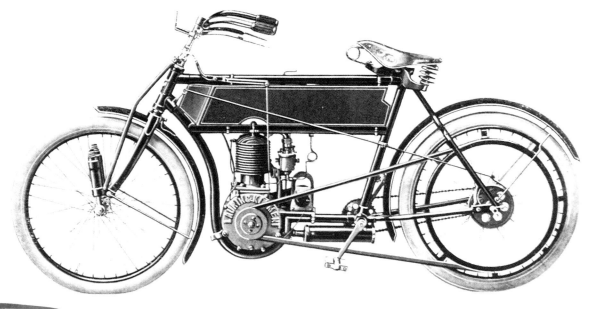

Laurin and Klement, Type BZ. The Prague constructors, like many others, considered racing to be the best form of advertisement. Leading riders included their patron, Count Kolowrat, Vondrich, Toman and Merfeit. Motorcycle production was discontinued in 1908. Laurin and Klement were made under licence in Germany under the Germania trademark.

the neutralised portions, the crowds were very thick. Here the competitors had to slacken speed and follow a cyclist, who piloted each one through. If any competitor passed the pilot he was liable to be disqualified. The course comprised a circuit of 33½ miles, and was covered five times, which equals slightly over 167½ miles.

Just before seven, the trumpet rang out announcing the arrival of the first competitor. French hopes soared high. Was it Lamberjack? He started first. Had he held his position? No? He had been passed by the Austrian, Vaslaw Vondrick, who, on his Laurin-Klement, was going splendidly. He passed the post amid loud and prolonged applause. Several minutes now went by before Petersen, the Dane, dashed up, then came Rignold on the Lagonda, third.

Following on Rignold's heels came Demester, Inghilbert, Toman, Mraz and Lamberjack.

Lamberjack told us that he had punctured several times, and he declared the road was strewn with nails.

The control at Dourdan now presented the appearance of an open-air kitchen. Here and there cooking operations were in full swing, everyone was refreshing the inner man. Meanwhile, Tampier tranquilly smoked on.

Varsity match, Brooklands, 1910. Motorcycle racing flourished at the Weybridge track and took on an accepted pattern: one-hour races, record time trials and individual attemps to establish national and world records were sprinkled with Oxford and Cambridge 'Inter-Varsity' meetings.

S. Bailey's Douglas, uses Sam Wright's Humber as a windshield in the 1912 Junior TT. The Douglas, running consistently and emitting a roar resembling a rotary aero engine, finished the winner. As a *finale*, Bailey carried off the three-hour record.

At the end of the second round the Austrian, Vondrick, was still first, going regularly. He was followed by Demester, who was gaining on him.

Petersen, who made the fastest time in the first round, had been delayed by a puncture. Rignold had punctured so many times that he gave up in disgust, whilst Silver, after five punctures, also decided the fates were against him.

Soon after Dourdan, Demester went to the front, and now held first place. The regular speed kept up by Demester was remarkable, and, bar accidents, the cup was practically at his mercy. Demester was never headed, and

arrived at the post first in 3h 43m 43s. The cup, therefore, goes to France.

Demester punctured twice in the first and second rounds, and decided to stop and fit his arrache clous – a device intended to draw nails out of tyres. After attaching these very useful accessories he travelled very fast. Toman (Laurin Klement), Austria, was second. He had three punctures, and broke his pedal chain. Inghilbert (Griffon), France, who was third, had two punctures, and broke his driving belt.

The race was a great success, and it is very much to be regretted that the British contingent were robbed of any chance of

The pioneer motorcycle racing fraternity – essentially young speed aspirants in breeches and high-necked jerseys – getting started at the Brooklands August meeting in 1910.

33

scoring by the puncture demon, who was very much in evidence. The Austrian firm of Laurin Klement showed up well, although they did not win. They took second and fifth places, and it is a good performance to finish in front of two of the redoubtable Griffons, which swept all before them in the eliminating trial.

AN AMERICAN HEAD PROTECTOR

Like the practical people they are, the Americans have recently designed a head protector for the use of racing motor cyclists. It is made of several thicknesses of soft leather, coming well down over the forehead and neck, and also provided with huge bulging ear caps, which, though they project a somewhat unhandsome manner on either side of the head, at the same time provide an excellent protection against concussion in case of a fall. We may mention that this form of head-dress has been made compulsory by the authorities governing motor cycle racing in America, and we cannot help thinking that our own authorities might do worse than follow this example.

ROUND THE TRACK
by P. J. Wallace

There was a marked expansion of the amateur element at Brooklands as a consequence of the introduction of motor-cycle racing, also bringing in its trail a broadening of the social context of the course. The May meeting of 1908 had been embellished by a handicap race exclusively confined to officers of HM Household Brigade of Guards; an event which might not have been so easily arranged had the entrants been required to compete on two wheels instead of four.

Sheer economics and the structure of society which distinguished the times had rendered inevitable a particular form of snobbery attaching to motor racing in the early days – exemplified by the posters proclaiming and inviting patronage from "the right people".

The introduction of motor-cycle racing was to change all that and was to make Brooklands, for the rest of its life, an open society requiring no other passport but a passionate interest in speed.

Motor-cars found their original market through their obvious advantages over the "carriage-and-pair" which had so long been the means of transport and a status symbol of both aristocracy and the leisured classes in general. It was inevitable that some of the trappings of social precedence should be reflected in the new sport of motor-racing. On the other hand, the origins of motor-cycle racing had been plebeian to a degree, tarnished by excessive intimacy with "trade". "Trade" may be interpreted as the very antithesis of the aristocratic idea.

Rain stops play: the scene in the paddock at Brooklands, Easter Monday, 1920, when bad weather was the cause of the postponement of the first post-war meeting. More motorcycle events were held at the Weybridge 'saucer' than any other type. Handicapping first appeared in 1908 and the following year saw the formation of the British Motor Cycle Racing Club ('Bemsee').

The traditional custom whereby a gentleman indulged in horse-racing by the nomination of a professional jockey to do the actual riding was easily carried over into the field of motor-racing. No such tradition has ever existed whereby a gentleman owned a number of pedal-cycles and hired professional cyclists to ride them in competition. However, members of the cycle trade did exactly that. For cycle-racing on the road was a highly respectable sport in which all classes of people could take part without any loss of status. The introduction of the "Safety Cycle" was followed by cut-throat competition between the various manufacturers. Each manufacturer sought the maximum advertisements of his products, but soon found that road-races through tracts of open countryside did not offer much opportunity.

Accordingly, they turned to the small wood-boarded tracks where competitors circled in full view of large concentrations of people. Unfortunately, this form of cycle-racing soon became a hot - bed of doubtful practice and open to the sort of corruption and chicanery which the horse-racing aristocracy, whatever their faults, would never have tolerated. It was in these inauspicious circumstances that motor-cycle racing made its debut; not by way of direct competition but in the form of pacing machines in whose slip-stream a pedal-cyclist was able to attain fantastic speeds.

It did not take long to conceive the idea of races between the pace-makers; but these were big and clumsy machines deliberately designed to produce maximum disturbance

Close company: advertisement for Continental Tyres. By 1911 the best ideas of the previous decade were developed and firmly established. The motorcycle had truly arrived.

Douglas, a Bristol firm, family owned until 1932, and remembered for their high-quality flat-twin engines, owed much of their success to their chief development rider, Freddy Dixon.

Douglas
Still "Leader of the Pack"

STILL LEADING——
The E.W. Douglas
has been established as Britain's Best Motorcycle—many

(and therefore resistance) of the air. Soon there were brought to these boarded tracks machines closely resembling the standard types offered for sale to the public. From the beginning, this new form of racing remained entirely free from malpractice if only because, quite unlike the pedal-cycle industry, the individual makers were for the most part modest men in a small way of business. Moreover, instead of hiring other people they rode the machines themselves.

Just as Napier cars had threatened to dominate the field of car-racing so, over much the same period, Matchless motor-cycles were predominant in their own sphere. These machines were manufactured by the firm of Collier & Sons. It was the sons "C. R." and "H. A." who swept the board at the first motorcycle race meeting at Brooklands by winning at something over 70mph on their own make of machine. There was nothing surprising in this: they were used to winning races, from the boarded track at Canning Town to the Tourist Trophy Races in the Isle of Man.

Both were fearless riders and sound engineers into the bargain. They were also physically tough, as they had to be to survive the violent buffetings of machines completely devoid of any springing. "Spring Forks" for

front wheels were already on the market, but these still young veterans of the board track (where they were not really necessary) would as yet have none of them, believing that they would result in too great a loss of transverse rigidity. Once again, Brooklands was to teach its lessons; sprung front-forks were very soon universal.

The number of starters in a Brooklands race might be as few as five or as many as 50; with the larger fields a simultaneous standing start provided an awe-inspiring spectacle to spectators and riders alike. Before 1914, clutches and gear-boxes were nearly unknown on motor-cycles, the rear wheel being driven directly by the engine through the medium of a rubber and canvas belt.

It was this mechanical austerity which compelled the rider to push and run along-side the machine with the exhaust valve lifted from its seating in order to reduce resistance from cylinder compression. When sufficient speed had been attained, the exhaust control-lever would be released and, with luck, the engine would burst into life. At this point, and not a moment later (otherwise the han-dle-bars might be wrenched from his grasp), the rider would leap into the air and vault into the saddle. Failure of the engine to fire could reduce the rider to a stage of physical exhaustion. High compression-ratio, big valve-overlaps and large-bore chokes all combined to make starting more difficult and uncertain; yet all three were required for maximum speed.

In my first race I was positioned near the middle of some 30 or 40 competitors spaced across the whole 100ft width of the track at

Crossing the burning heath: an artist's interpretation of a dangerous crossing for rider and passenger following a drought.

39

the Fork, and I tensely awaited the signal to start. Away to the left and in front stood A. V. Ebblewhite, chief-starter and time-keeper; his left-arm was extended horizontally and in his hand was a small flag; the dropping of this flag would be the signal to go.

Although I had never been round the circuit before, the possibility of any surprises being in store never occurred to me, so intensely had the situation been imagined. The correct technique was believed to be simple enough – to get away smartly and make a bee-line for the inner edge of the track; the closer one got, the shorter the distance to be covered The present race was for a 100 miles, the equivalent of 37 laps.

At last the flag dropped and immediately the scene was transformed. Three dozen young men were heaving their heavy machines forward and running as fast as they could go. In a very few seconds there was bedlam; first a few, one after another, and then the whole mass of engines burst into life. As the riders leapt into their saddles, motor-cycles swerved dangerously close to one another and for a few moments a number of collisions seemed inevitable. As my own engine sprang into life the competitor on the right swerved in front, missing my wheel by inches as he made towards the inside.

For my own part, once safely in the saddle all thought of the inside line vanished into thin air; it was one thing to know the correct procedure, it was another to carry it out. Quite apart from the fact that everybody displayed the same intention, my machine bucked about in the most unexpected manner and every effort was required to keep it on a straight course.

The difficulties were accentuated by the need to juggle with the pair of levers which controlled the carburettor. It was not simply a matter of opening the throttle. Motor-cycle carburettors possessed both a throttle lever and another lever which controlled the

Line-up for the Brooklands August meeting, 1910. By the time this photograph was taken, the motor-cycle was no longer a new invention and for many it represented a form of sport and social enjoyment.

strength of the petrol/air mixture. Then there was the ignition advance-and-retard lever, this one situated on the side of the petrol tank about which my knees were tightly gripped, otherwise it would have been impossible to remove one hand from the handlebars.

As we climbed the one in thirty incline towards the curve round the Members' Hill, most were doing about 50mph but varying our speeds sufficiently to space ourselves out: the inside edge was now becoming more accessible. Still much disconcerted to find the going so rough, I settled down to take things as they came. There was not long to wait. Sweeping round the long bend and under the Members' Bridge, all the time the way overshadowed by the high Members' Banking on the right and the hill on the left, I became aware of going downhill as the speed rose perceptibly.

Emerging from this wide ravine, there came into view the whole vast expanse of Brooklands, the Railway Straight commencing in the immediate foreground and stretching far ahead. It was an inspiring sight and a memorable moment; it was only a second later when it became yet more memorable but distinctly less inspiring. There came a sudden thrust from the left and in response the machine veered to the right, accompanied by a wobbling of the front wheel and handlebars. I was in a cold sweat, heightened by the attainment of maximum speed (about 65mph) as the bottom of the one in twenty-five incline was passed. Beginning the long straight beside the railway embankment the machine became stable and the bumps less troublesome .

The temporary deviation had been caused by sudden exposure to a southwest wind on emerging from the shelter of the Members' Hill. The strength of the wind that day was relatively light, its effect much exaggerated by my own stupidity. It was a requirement of regulations that motorcycles should carry on

41

each side a circular disc of 12in diameter, painted black and bearing the competitors number in bold white figures. A man with a brush and bucket of whitewash was posted in the Paddock for this particular duty. In my inexperience I had bolted my number-plates to the front-forks, with the result that even a moderate wind-pressure had produced a marked turning-moment on the front wheel assembly.

It may be added that when a really strong southwest wind was blowing the sudden impact could be a considerable hazard no matter where the number-plates might be situated; to the unwary even a racing-car was not immune.

The journey down the Railway Straight was not marked by any similarly untoward event; which was just as well because there was plenty to contend with. The motorcycles of those days depended upon the timely operation of a hand-pump for their lubrication; failure in its proper operation could result in engine seizure, causing in turn a serious skid or even the propulsion of the rider over the handlebars. At touring speeds one pumpful every ten miles would normally be sufficient; at racing speeds, very much more because so much oil was thrown out of the exhaust pipe.

Without experience, which might be bought dearly, it was difficult to decide how many pumpfuls should be given during each lap; too little would mean seizure, too much would oil up the sparking-plug. It was a difficult decision to take for quite a different reason: operation of the pump meant taking one hand off the handlebars. It was not too bad when the pump was fitted with a non-return valve and the plunger returned under the action of a spring; one hand was required for only a few seconds in one single operation. The more common case of a simple pump, worked in conjunction with a hand-operated two-way cock and requiring four consecutive operations extending over 20 seconds, could be a veritable nightmare. Hitting a bad bump with one hand off the handlebars was a combination of events to be avoided.

THE TRIUMPH GIRL

After the Railway Straight came the long, almost semi-circular curve of the Byfleet Banking; it seemed almost interminable. Soon the aeroplane sheds and hangers were visible just beyond the inside edge. Then came the narrow bridge over the track which gave access to the flying-ground; after that had been passed the circuit was monotonous apart from the discomfort. At last, the banking came to an end and the Fork could be seen ahead. Its passing would register the end of the first lap. As all the asides will have tended to distortion of the time-scale, it should be mentioned that this lap had taken just less than three minutes.

Being in line and usually close to the inner edge, one saw little ahead beyond the man immediately in front except on the Byfleet Banking, where it was possible to see across to a few riders curving off to the left. During the first lap I was overtaken by one or two whose get-away had been even slower than my own; it was only after a few more laps that the really fast machines came by

TRIUMPH
stets fahrbereit

TRIUMPH WERKE === NÜRNBERG A·G.

after completing one more lap than myself. The race included several classes of engine ranging from 250cc to 1,000cc twins.

At about the ninth or tenth lap, apart from feeling tired, I had really settled down, but without warning there came a stunning blow on my back, my machine went into a skid and stopped almost abruptly. The driving-belt had broken and become wedged between the belt-rim and a rear tubular member of the frame – it was this jamming which had caused the skid and allowed the free end of the belt to hit me in the back.

Not only had the belt broken, but one half of the fastener had become stuck in the groove of the engine pulley; in consequence, the spare belt entwined about my middle was useless. There was nothing to be done except to walk, pushing the machine all the way to the Fork.

Far and away the fastest competitor was Arthur Moorhouse riding a 1,000cc Indian twin; with unfailing regularity he would pass about halfway up the banking although his speed was not more than about 75mph. In the course

of this race he was to break the existing one-hour record. At the next meeting, the following month, he met his death along the Railway Straight by hitting a telegraph post in which remained the imprint made by the impact of his goggles. The cause was never established although it may be surmised: despite the fact that Indians were fitted with automatic mechanical lubrication of the engine, an automatic (single control) carburettor, its throttle operated (as in the case of ignition advance/retard) by twist-grips instead of awkward levers, Moorhouse was in the habit of riding with only one hand on the handlebars while he fiddled with something or other on his engine.

By the time the Fork had been reached, I was in company with a number of other unfortunates pushing their machines. The pushers were an assorted lot, two professionals and the rest amateurs, one little older than myself, all of them inspired by the indomitable spirit of Brooklands, the determination to try again and do better next time.

THE MOTOR CYCLE AND ITS DEVELOPMENT
by Frederick A Talbot

The motorcycle has always been considered a lonely means of travelling; that is, in its essential form. Brilliant efforts have been made to provide the rider with the comfort of a travelling companion, by means of trailers, fore-carriages, sociables, and side-cars; but they cannot be construed into more than mere makeshifts, while many of these auxiliaries are a source of danger both to the occupant and to the cyclist, and the machine undeniably rides better without them. At the same time they are highly convenient and much appreciated by those who are content to jog along the high roads at a moderate speed, but a great number of adherents to this lure of automobilism are rather apt to indulge in a "joy-ride", and consider clipping along the highway at anything over 25mph to be the only real pleasure in motorcycling.

Triumph catalogue, 1930. German-built Triumph motorcycles used mainly British-made engines and parts. When the marriage between Triumph in Nuremburg and Triumph in Coventry was dissolved, German Triumph took the names Orial and TWN, while the English Triumph was known as TEC (Triumph Engineering Company).

43

DIANA AWHEEL
by Betty and Nancy Debenham

Motorcycling is becoming more and more popular amongst women, but there are still many timid souls who hesitate to take the first step to this freedom which so many of us enjoy. This seems all the more sad when we consider that no girl that we have ever met who has once sampled the joys of motorcycling willingly has given it up.

It is this initial step that seems so difficult, but really it is not, because the machine that appears to be – and is – so full of power and speed, is absolutely docile, even in the hands of a novice. Granted some idea of balance (it is always as well to learn to ride an ordinary cycle first), the control of a motorcycle is easily acquired if one chooses a quiet road, or a park, for one's first venture.

It certainly is wise to choose a lightweight, at any rate to begin with. A small engine is very much easier to start than a large one, a most important point for the novice. There is nothing more discouraging than to "kick" and "kick" at an irresponsive engine, with lookers-on increasing in number until in despair one wheels the machine round the corner to try again in comparative privacy.

One has none of that unhappiness with a small engine. One slight depression of the kick-starter and, usually, away she goes. To the uninitiated this may seem an unimportant

Opposite: Laurin and Klement, BD.
At the turn of the century it was hardly considered proper for a woman to motor at all. The years immediately following the First World War witnessed a revival in the desire for personal transport and saw young ladies take to the road in significant numbers.

Naptha Soap.
By the beginning of the twenties, women were no longer unwilling to go on a motorcycle, encouraging the growth of the industry and the evolution of larger machines in addition to the lighter solo.

45

One of the oldest names in motor-cycling, Royal Enfield competed officially in races and a 996cc V-twin with ohv JAP racing engine, ridden by E. Magner of Sweden, broke the world speed record for sidecar outfits over one mile.

Pillion passengers made an appearance circa 1910. Men would usually sit astride a cushion tied to the carrier; ladies would be carried side-saddle. This common, but hazardous, practice was outlawed around 1930. Women began to sit astride and manufacturers to supply proper pillion saddles, and later, dual seats. Brooks held a virtual monopoly in the manufacture of saddles in Britain.

46

THE FAMOUS 6 H.P. ROYAL ENFIELD.

lines with plenty of pockets, rather after the style of an army officer's tunic. We find that corduroy wears splendidly and does not show the dirt, or, if one is inclined to go to a little more expense, Burberry material is excellent.

A light and warm woolly jumper with a polo neck and a pull-on cap to match are cosy adjuncts, also a poncho or a leatherette coat in case of rain. We find that flat-heeled Russian boots are very good for motor-cycling, and they are most useful for slipping on in a hurry, if one is only going a short dis-tance, and a frock is preferred. It is a simple matter to tie a pair of shoes on the carrier; upon arrival a quick change can be made, and – there we are, all complete, without any disfiguring road stains on our silk stockings.

Overalls are most useful for slipping on over summer frocks when it is too much of a performance to don breeches. The spat-feet

point to labour, but it is one of the things that make all the difference between comfort and misery to the potential rider. We know it is knack to a great extent that is required to start the bigger models. But who amongst us, when essaying a new art, is possessed of knack in connection with it ?

Riding position is very important; it is advisable to have the saddle so low that both feet easily can be placed flat upon the ground. This enhances the feeling of security considerably, and also is infinitely more rest-ful on long journeys. It allows for change of position much more than when perched up high, and prevents unnecessary strain in reaching the handlebars.

Clothes too, make a tremendous differ-ence. Correctly garbed, one feels one can conquer anything. From our varied experi-ence we have been able to make a selection which, we think, combines a certain amount of smartness with comfort. It comprises breeches and coat, the latter cut on roomy

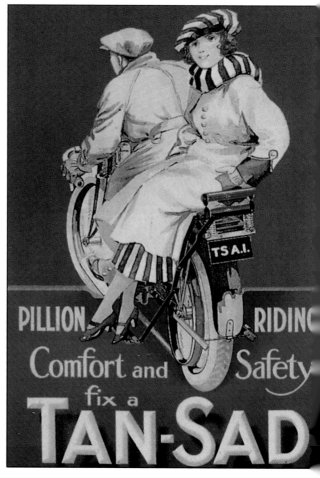

PILLION RIDING
Comfort and Safety
fix a
TAN-SAD

Sidecars came to be used by the army during the First World War for the rapid movement of senior officers when roads were too poor for the use of staff cars. AC, Morgan, GWK and others devised heavier sidecar-type machines which were built as a unit. After the war, the increasing desire to get out and about led to a greater demand for a comfortable second, and third, seat.

Neckarsulm Strick-maschinen Union, one of the prominent German constructors, assembled their machines at Neckarsulm. They won big races, broke many international records and proved again and again the excellence of their design. Walter Moore, the eminent British designer, who had created the first Norton ohc machine in 1927, joined the works and produced *inter alia* fast, Norton-like ohc singles.

Champion spark plugs advertisement. Machines were available in all sizes to suit all tastes. Those in the middle range were the most common; the smaller machines – too light and underpowered to carry a pillion seat or sidecar – were in some degree of minority. Towards the end of the twenties, with the ever-improving efficiency of the smaller engines, the popularity of the smallest machines increased.

protect the shoes and ankles, and a roomy raincoat hides the frock tucked into the tops.

It is well to remember that however warm the day, it is always cooler on a motorcycle than one expects. Therefore, the wise girl turns out warmly, even if lightly, clad. Silk is marvellous for resisting cold, and a silk blouse underneath her jumper should make the most shivery of mortals happier.

Lots of people ask us how we keep our skin from peeling, with so much exposure to wind and rain. The answer to that is "cold cream". It is most unwise to wash with soap and water after a long ride. However tempting the idea of a good wash, it is much better to remove the dust and dirt with plentiful supplies of cold cream, finishing up, perhaps,

by just dipping the face in cold water. A liberal dusting of powder before setting off again is a protection.

Diana can ride all the year round if she makes a few simple preparations for any temperature and weather. Warm handlebar muffs, lined with fur, are a boon in winter. A really good pair will keep the hands warm and cosy in the coldest weather, and they are invaluable for keeping the gloves dry in the sudden thunder-storms we are often favoured with in the middle of summer.

So let Diana take her courage in both hands and purchase her ideal machine. She will be well recompensed by the countless happy days she will spend in the saddle.

The premier tyre company, Dunlop were a part of motorcycling
history from the earliest days.

VIVE LE SPORT

"The Spirit of the Time shall teach me speed."

"King John" William Shakespeare

THE GREAT RACE 1911
by Arthur M. Ritz

The greatest race in the motorcycle world, "The International Tourist Trophy Race", conducted by the Auto Cycle Union on the Isle of Man, off the coast of England, has been won by an Indian Motorcycle; and not only this, but two other Indian machines took the second and third places as well.

Such a performance has never been equalled, not even in the races of previous years, where the distance was not only much shorter but also over a far easier course than that traversed in the event of the present year.

To succeed in such an undertaking a motorcycle must possess not one good quality alone, but every quality that can be asked of a motorcycle, under every conceivable condition. The motor must develop wonderful power, and continue to do so under most adverse conditions. A stop to cool down is impossible, and the machine must go on continually with undiminished speed.

The endurance, not only of the motor, but of every part must be everlasting. The failure of a screw would be fatal. The control must be simple in the extreme, easy and certain in its operation, and instant in action. The doings of these Indians was a modern miracle, and a wonderful demonstration of cunning designing, clever combinations of materials, and precision of workmanship.

The object of the race, as officially stated, "is intended to assist the development of an ideal touring motorcycle of the power required by the ordinary user, regardless of the number of cylinders. It is not intended for racing motorcycles, and is not necessarily a race between existing standard types."

The Hendee Manufacturing Company entered five twin cylinder Indians for the race, exact duplicates of the regular twin machines except in the reduced size of the cylinders. As the course was a very hilly one, they were fitted with the regular Indian two speed gear and free engine clutch.

The course included Snaefell Mountain, a very sizable elevation, the length of which is in the neighbourhood of four miles. Besides the mountain, there were a number of lesser hills but with trying grades, and this circuit had to be made five times.

Such a course is evidently a most severe test, not only of power, but of endurance and reliability, and the winner must make the entire distance with absolutely no stop except the regular ones for gasoline.

For this race 59 machines started, and only 28 survived. Such a wiping out of machines especially prepared to meet known conditions is the best evidence of the test. The result of the race was a wonderful victory for the Indian, for the first man in was O.C. Godfrey, one of the leading Indian riders.

The second to finish was C.R. Collier, on a Matchless, a rider who has competed in

these events since their inception, and who has been twice a winner and finished once in second place. Collier's long experience on the course and special study of conditions have always given him and his machine a great advantage, and to beat Collier on a Matchless gives a man an enviable standing in England.

The third man in was C.B. Franklin, riding an Indian, and the fourth was A.J. Moorhouse, also mounted on an Indian, and he wins the honour of being the first private owner to finish. All of these men rode very carefully, and the regularity with which they made their circuits was highly commented on by the spectators as an indication of the splendid construction and reliability of their machines.

Jake de Rosier, who had gone to England to take part in this race, came in twelfth, but he had encountered hard luck,

and his performance was most creditable. During his practice riding on the course he had six severe falls, which did not leave him in any too good condition for the great trial. In the race he was leader of the first lap, but dropped back a little on the second, and on the third had a fall which nearly put him out of commission. He really was in a dazed condition, and it required great nerve to keep on riding as he did, and finish the entire course.

J.R. Alexander, the fifth Indian entered, was the twentieth man home, but was really the hero of the team. In rounding a bend in the road he came upon another rider falling directly in front of him. This brought Alexander down, and he stripped everything from one side of his machine and sustained a terrible cut on his knee. Not withstanding this, he got his machine started again and completed the lap, with his leg dangling,

53

De Rosier versus Collier. The great tradition of the Tourist Trophy was born in 1907. A major influence on the motorcycle movement, the uphill and downhill sections, plus dozens of corners, made up this most demanding of road racing courses and provided a proving ground for all aspects of technical design.

Indian, 1911. Bicycle king George Hendee and a Swedish-born Brooklyn tool and die maker named Hedstrom joined in a partnership to design and produce one of the foremost names in the development of the motorcycle. Indians were of very advanced design and the Springfield factory built a variety of racing machines. Indian riders were either employed by the works or rode for dealers who, in many countries, were issued with racing machines from the factory for publicity purposes.

Vauxhall, 1920. A rare motorcycle from the Vauxhall Company, which started manufacturing motor cars in 1903. The fluted tank was unique to the Luton firm, which was finally absorbed by General Motors.

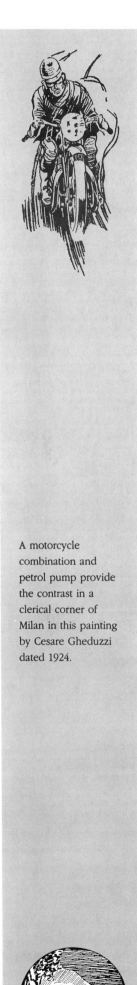

before fitting his extra foot rests.

In the meantime he had to hang onto his ignition connection with one hand as it had been detached from the handle bar by his fall. Owing to his insecure position he sustained a second fall before the end of the lap, which broke his rear mud-guard containing the nail catcher, and afterwards he had two punctures in his rear tyre. Even with all these mishaps and delays, he was not the last man to finish, and he brought his machine home, making a clean score for the Indian team.

the race at unauthorized controls, and as this was in direct violation of the rules protests were sustained, and Collier was disqualified.

De Rosier lost the bag containing all his tools and spare parts in the second round, and when he damaged his machine in his fall he had nothing to repair with, and one of his spark plugs was out of commission. He had to ride three miles on one cylinder, to the next control, but as he desired to have the credit of finishing the race, he got spare parts and tools from his attendants, fixed his machine and continued.

A motorcycle combination and petrol pump provide the contrast in a clerical corner of Milan in this painting by Cesare Gheduzzi dated 1924.

The road conditions, from an English point of view, are described as very bad, and even de Rosier, who knows something of American roads, remarked: "This race ain't going to be no tea party". The elimination and retirement of more than half of the machines fully corroborates de Rosier's opinion.

When the reports of the marshals came in, it was found that Collier had taken on gasoline and received assistance twice during

The delay of the accident had, of course, lost him all chance of first place, and the necessity of accepting outside assistance disqualified him according to the rules, but he still has the satisfaction of having finished, which made a clean score for the Indian team, Collier's disqualification giving the first three places in the race to Indians ridden by Godfrey, Franklin, and Moorhouse.

It was a great victory well worth the running and well worth the winning.

Pratts' alcohol-based racing ethyl was the preferred choice of speedmen. The early petrol engine worked on the same principle as those of today, but carburettor and ignition systems were rather unreliable. Towards the end of the first decade of this century petrol engines became much more efficient, with spray or jet carburettors taking over completely from their surface or wick forebears.

AN AMERICAN VICTORY
"Motor Cycling" 1911

All motorcycling roads led to Brooklands last Saturday, where the champions of England and America were to meet in a series of three matches, over distances of two, five and ten laps. As 3 o'clock drew near, the excitement became intense, and when the two great rivals appeared a crowd at once collected round each man, who, waiting with their machines, received the good wishes for success from their friends.

Jake de Rosier said that, though he was not confident of winning, he was going to do his best. He was very pleased with the way his Indian was running. His back tyre was a new Blue Streak, with a six ply tread, the front one having only four plies. He put this new cover on as the one he had been using the previous week was slightly worn. Except for this change, de Rosier assured us that his

machine was in exactly the same condition as when he broke three world records the previous Saturday.

The engine is fitted with auxiliary exhaust ports drilled in the cylinder, and the exhaust pipes are only 3 inches long, and discharge straight into the open air. A present to him of a pair of knee grips was secured to the tank, and this is a wrinkle he has picked up over here. He finds them most comfortable, and they give him a greater sense of security. He has discarded his narrow handlebars in favour of a wider pair, as the narrow ones are difficult to steer with on a bumpy track like Brooklands. Jake says his back wheel is

thrown so high off the ground that it spins around in mid-air, and distance is lost accordingly. He used Pratt's petrol and Wakefield oil.

Charles Collier had a beautiful spick-and-span Matchless. There were no auxiliary exhausts, but the long exhaust pipes had the shells of silencers on them. An Amac carburettor fed Pratt's spirit to the engine, and Hutchinson tyres were shod to the wheels. The Matchless spring fork was used, and Vacuum oil lubricated the engine bearings.

But the race! It is impossible to do it justice, so magnificent a spectacle did these two giants, battling out the greatest motorcycle warfare ever seen, present. At the start, Harry Collier wheeled his brother's machine down to the far end by the bridge over the Wey, and Garret did the like with the Indian, while the two rivals walked down together, chatting to one another. The starter's car was also there, and presently it was seen that all three were coming nearer; faster and faster they went until, when the two competitors were dead in line, down went the red flag in the car, and the race was begun. They crossed the line together, with "C.R." perhaps a shade ahead.

The exuberant feelings of the crowd gave vent in cheer after cheer, the bookmakers

Harry Reed, Percy Butler and, to the right, Arthur Moorhouse. Indian were the racing champions during the early days and the big red bikes won races galore, including the 1911 Isle of Man Senior TT road race, where they scored an epic 1-2-3 victory. George M. Holley, another pioneer manufacturer, recalling his first place in the Boston to New York race in 1901, said: 'That was quite a ride. Cobblestones, mud, sand, chickens and people, but the engine kept purring and I arrived right on schedule. Of course, with the layer of mud and dust on my face even my own mother wouldn't have recognised me'.

Two of the quickest: brothers Harry and Charlie Collier, who rode Matchless motorcycles made by their family. The brothers brought the London marque to international prominence through their racing success and, following Indian's stunning 1-2-3 win on the Island, challenged their ace rider, Jake de Rosier, to a three-race match at the Brooklands oval.

Far from the madding crowd. The period between the two wars saw the worldwide expansion of personal transport. At the Annual Show, held at Olympia in London, the variety of types and diversity of motorcycle designs seemed endless, and not every make could be accommodated.

shouted louder than ever, and two small dots flashed out of sight round the hill. A few seconds elapsed, and then they came out from under the bridge, and were 100 yards beyond before the sound of their exhausts reached the listening ears of those at the fork. Jake was a couple of lengths behind, but began to close the gap quickly.

They went out of sight again down the straight, and, when next viewed by the aero sheds, the Englishman was 10 yards ahead. They tore past the judge's box with Jake taking Collier's shelter, but, on leaving the big banking, the Indian got a wheel ahead for a few seconds. The Matchless, however, quickened up, and was in front at the aero sheds, and came into the straight first. Then came a most magnificent piece of riding by Jake, for he suddenly dashed away, and, before Charlie could quicken up, had got to the front.

Collier tucked his head down lower and made a final spurt, but it was too late, for, although he seemed to be catching up quickly, the Indian crossed the line first, though there was not daylight between them. It was a splendid finish, and both men came in for a lot of cheering, and, though the majority of the spectators would rather have seen the Englishman win, the splendid riding of the American called for admiration from Briton and Yankee alike.

The second race was five laps, and again a very level start was made. Collier made the pace very hot at first and led, amid the frenzied shrieks of the crowd, who were now dead set on him winning this race and drawing level. Past the judge's box for the first time they both struck two bad bumps, and Jake wobbled badly. It was very noticeable, however, that, whereas Collier rode very straight indeed, de Rosier by no means fol-

Round the Island. The Isle of Man, off the west coast of England, allowed racing on its roads and in 1907 played host to the Auto Cycle Club's first Tourist Trophy Race. The rules of the TT required that standard touring models be used and under its spell the motorcycle, especially the British version, flourished.

lowed a perfectly straight line. Perhaps this was because the atmosphere behind Collier was changeable, owing to the draughts created by the leading rider and machine.

Whatever it was, it was remarkable, for, looked at from in front, one could see the Englishman coming towards one riding perfectly straight, while every now and then the little, crouched-up figure on the Indian would appear first at one side and then at the other, though he never for a second deserted that

back wheel of the Matchless. It was great – it was magnificent! At 80 miles an hour this masterpiece of American track riding was sucking away at the power of the Matchless, letting his rival draw him along in the vortex that his wild rush through the air created.

Down the railway stretch, with the wind behind, the speed must have been 90mph. Though the crowd yelled madly and joyously every time Collier passed them ahead of his rival, the wiseacres shook their heads, for

they knew who was doing the pacing work. So the tearing, roaring race went on.

Suddenly a shout, then a wild yell as a babble of voices shriek, "Where's Jake?" He is stopping on the far side of the track. "What has happened?" Then a British cheer as the Matchless sweeps past on its last lap. "Has his engine seized?" "Jake's given up." These are the hysterical remarks bandied from mouth to mouth. A few more moments of suspense, and the English champion roared home the

victor to a deafening storm of applause from the supporters of home industries.

Then slowly up the track is seen the worthy Jake carefully picking his way, with foot extended, and, trailing on the ground, caught between the spokes and the right fork, is his front cover, and dangling from the hub are a few shreds of what had one been a tube. Yes, riding on the rim, with not a scrap of rubber between the metal and the track, came the tough little man from over the

In celebration – chairing R. Weatherall, the winner of the Brooklands 100-Mile Race, riding a machine of his own make. Though the weather was threatening at midday, the giant handicap was actually run off in brilliant sunshine.

water, and, with never a word of anger or annoyance, explained that his tyre had suddenly burst, and the cover come off the rim. Think of it! At 80 miles an hour, Jake the redoubtable held up his racer when the tyre left the rim. "Miraculous!" "Incredible!" were the expressions used by the racing men when they had fully grasped the meaning of it all.

One match each and one to go. What better sport could be hoped for? The wired on Blue Streak was cut off the wheel by Jake's orders, the wheel extracted and another front wheel, shod with a Continental, substituted for it.

The final had now to be run off, and all was ready for the start when it was discovered that the Indian machine was loose as to some of its nuts, so that a spanner had to be procured, for these racers do not carry toolbags. Then, after a false start, it was ascertained that the trailing cover had broken one

of the carbon brushes in Jake's magneto, so another journey had to be made to get another one.

Off at last. What a shout! What terrific excitement among the crowd is now caused by these two machines rapidly gaining speed – speed so abnormal that before everyone was aware that these two motorcycling giants had really started on their great deciding battle their engines were roaring under the bridge, and in less time than it takes to write, they were back again past the judge's box, neck and neck, though, after taking the hill and the big banking, the wily Jake tucked in behind the Matchless once more!

In this order the second lap was run, but the sight of the little brown-clad man, with his leather helmet, on his great wobbling racer keeping less than a wheel's length behind his rival, sent many a thrill through those who saw him. The next lap it was Jake

Tourist Trophy: a road racing classic that vastly enriched racing history. In terms of effort, endurance and toughness, mental as well as physical, the Senior race has taken at least as much winning as any title in sport.

who crossed the line first, but Collier came down the straight 10 lengths ahead, and the over-hopeful Britishers shouted for joy. "C.R." did this half-mile in 84.8mph, but that relent-less Yankee racer was on his back tyre again at the aeroplane sheds.

Taking the big banking for the fifth time, Jake lost no distance, as he had previously done, and so the great race went on. But trouble was in store for the Englishman. His machine was missing badly. Glancing down, he saw what was the matter – the high-ten-sion wire had come off a plug, and though the engine conked on the hill, Collier never stopped, though he was barely able to keep going, and at last, in spite of shocks from the magneto, he got the errant wire in place and screwed the nut. But he had lost fully a mile, and there were but four more laps to go. It was quite pathetic to see this great champion trying to make up time lost for such a trifling cause, and try he did.

Grand Prix de l'ACF des Motos at Amiens – Fenton (Clement), winner of the 350cc class.

When it came to the end of the seventh lap the little man in the airman's suit was but 20 seconds ahead, and he was looking behind him for quite long stretches to see where his opponent was. Looking round over his shoulder, without going out of his course and at 80 miles an hour! What a skill! What daring ! In this eighth lap the champion of the homeside came up on the machine of the American, but receded on the penultimate circuit. And so, without making a mistake, Jake de Rosier won the third race, the final, and the prize money.

Only one could win, and though Englishmen sympathized with their countryman, there was plenty of cheering for Jake, for he rode magnificently. C.R. Collier certainly did the pacing work, but after all it was a race to finish first, not to lead the whole way, and Jake, with his knowledge of track riding, was out to win. He nursed his engine by taking Collier's shelter, and he cannot be blamed for doing this. To say that both are magnificent riders is puerile: they are the two most magnificent riders the world has ever seen. Collier's steering was beautiful:

he kept a course as straight as an arrow. Jake rode very differently; he dodged about the whole time, and even looked as if he were quizzing his opponent sometimes when he would dash alongside him for a short distance.

The styles of racing, in this country and America, are quite different. Here Charlie Collier has never had to take anybody's dust, and he invariably gets ahead and stays there. Jake, on the other hand, rides behind his most dangerous rivals until the time comes for a final dash. Collier had his best chance in the first race, and had he gone all out round the last bend he might have done it, but he made that fatal mistake of letting the backmarker get his throttle open first when but a few seconds from the finish. Whether Jake was all out even then we cannot tell, as he says nothing. The Hutchinson tyres on the Matchless behaved splendidly, withstanding the terrific speed and appearing little worn at the finish.

Jake's hand was bleeding at the finish, the skin being chafed through, and his back and leggings were covered in oil, for what

67

Triumph of Coventry. The demand for a bike capable of pulling a sidecar and possibly carrying a pillion passenger as well, thus enabling the whole family to go motoring, led to the production of considerably larger machines.

oil, from the auxiliary exhaust ports, escaped his leggings went on to the back wheel and was immediately thrown up on to his back.

It is the opinion of the very best judges that there is not a difference of one mile an hour between the two machines, and this seems to be fully borne out by the results. Jake will presumably go back to America and sigh for more champions to conquer, but it is now certain that all doubt has been removed from the minds of those who were at one time disbelieving of the wonderful tales told of his prowess. He has beaten our records on our own track under our own timing, he has conquered our champion, and he has established a reputation for road racing in the few weeks that he has been here.

THE ONE AND ONLY...
A look back at the 1921 BMCRC 500 Mile Race at Brooklands By Cyril Posthumus

Proposals for a car race of this distance had first been made in 1914, and were revived soon after the first world war, but this bike event just "seemed to happen" with little advance campaigning. The organisers were the BMCRC, the big prize was the 200-guinea Miller Gold Cup, presented by Capt. Alistair G. Miller, and there were five capacity classes catering for just about everybody – 250cc, 350cc, 500cc, 750cc and 1,000cc. Despite the Isle of Man TT race held three weeks earlier, entries just poured in for the race on July 6th, 1921, 64 being accepted with a dozen late-comers as reserves.

With the exception of AJS and Scott, the cream of British bikes were there – Norton, Triumph, Zenith, Douglas, Matchless, Sunbeam, ABC, New Imperial and a dozen other makes. Not that this numerical supremacy guaranteed a British success, for the 1,000cc "big bike" class was a battle-ground for the two premier American makes, Indian and Harley-Davidson, which were very fast indeed.

As to the list of riders, it was full of names of fame and fame-to-be. Kaye Don was to

THE NEW MACHINE.
Sketched outside the "Swan's Nest" at Stratford-on-Avon, a famous rendezvous for motor-cyclists in the Midlands.

The new machine. By the middle 1920s in Europe the motor-cycle was enjoying tremendous popularity. Grand Prix road racing then became vitally important. Much of the knowledge gained from racing was applied to the standard roadsters.

Captain (later Sir) A. Miller, who succeeded to the title during a versatile racing career. Equally at home on two wheels or four, Miller was at one time Competition Manager for the Wolseley Motor Company. His companion is L.C.G. Le Champion, known for his exploits with monster aero-engined cars in the early twenties.

handle a big Zenith twin, A.E. Miller himself a similar Martin, E.B. Ware, a future "Morganatic", had a Sunbeam, Col. R.N. Stewart, husband of Gwenda Stewart, the great lady driver, and proprietor of the Trump concern, was riding a Trump-JAP, G.A. (Tolly) Vandervell of subsequent Vanwall GP car fame was down for a 490cc Norton, and a Brooklands novice named F.W. Dixon was to ride a 998cc Harley-Davidson.

Needless to say the principal Brooklands specialists were there – Herbert Le Vack, Vic Horsman, Claude Temple, Jack Woodhouse, Reuben Harveyson, O.M. Baldwin, Jack Emerson, D.R. O'Donovan, Frank Longman and others. With the vast field of 64 bikes spread out over the broad Finishing Straight early on a July morning, Brooklands seemed really to have "arrived", with a classic long-distance race unfolding for the first time.

For some odd reason the powers-that-be settled on 7am as starting time, and public attendance was naturally very sparse at that hour, although plenty came along later. Different classes were distinguished by differently coloured flimsy jackets over their leathers, and the noise as the vast pack of two-wheelers, all with wide-open exhausts, were released must have startled many local residents from their beds that fine Saturday morning. Quoting *The Motor Cycle*: "The sharp crack of so many well-tuned exhausts,

the clouds of Castrol mingling with the mists of early morning, the semi-comic aspect of so many running and leaping men, formed a spectacle which repaid the company for its early rising."

It was a long, hard race, with bikes running at full throttle on a rough and bumpy track, and attrition soon set in. The big Harleys and Indians were quickly out in front and at each other's throats, leaving behind a wake of trouble as the pace, the weather, engines and tyres all grew hotter. Jack Emerson's Douglas had valve rocker trouble, Kaye Don's Anzani-engined Zenith and S.C. Woodhouse's spring-framed Matchless cooked plugs. A.G. Miller, donor of the premier award, broke a fuel pipe on his Martin twin, and Harry Reed's big twin ohv JAP threw first its back tyre, and then its rider, when passing the Vickers shed at over 80mph.

Reed pluckily walked back, had his injuries dressed and resumed racing, until his tank, damaged in the crash, leaked all its fuel away. Then race-leader Herbert La Vack had the rear tyre on his Indian burst along the Railway Straight. He nursed his way round to the pits, where they didn't waste time removing the tyre but simply fitted a new wheel-and-tyre ready-inflated. The stop still cost him 6 seconds, giving D.H. Davidson's Harley-Davidson a 12-mile lead.

A.A. Prestwich (350cc Dot-JAP) and C. Sgonina (500cc Triumph Ricardo 4-valve) both went out with seized engines; F.G. Edmonds had tyre trouble on his side-valve Triumph; Claude Temple on a Harley-Davidson had both tyre and engine trouble and had to retire when lying third. Padley on a 500cc Blackburne misjudged his braking speed and sent several pit personnel scattering, and S.M. Greening came off his 350cc Coulsoll-B at speed and had to go to hospital. The 350cc flat-twin "Royal" Douglas entered by HRH The Duke of York (who later became George VI) and ridden by S.E. Wood threw a rear tyre, then broke a chain, and was finally disqualified for receiving unauthorised pit assistance.

Victor Horsman (real name Vincent Edward Horsman), principal Brooklands specialist. The Vickers aero sheds are in the background. Many classic meetings and record-breaking attempts took place at the banked Surrey course.

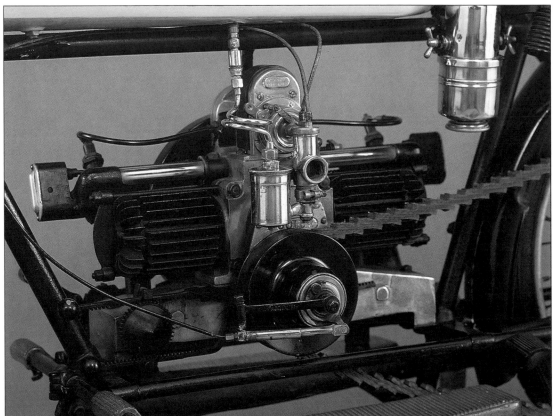

Wooler, 1920. John Wooler was a very individualistic designer, responsible for a number of unconventional machines. He built his first example in 1911 and was still designing motorcycles forty years on.

T.R. Allchin during a successful record attempt on a 998cc Harley-Davidson, Brooklands 1922. Harley-Davidson, a contemporary of Indian, was founded in 1901 by William Harley and Walter Davidson. The powerful 'thumpers' from Milwaukee were valued in road racing in Europe and speed hillclimbing and sprinting in Britain. Strangely enough, the most visible of U.S. manufacturers never produced a 4-cylinder model.

Next it was first-place-man Davidson's turn for tyre trouble, and Le Vack's Indian moved ahead again, followed by a chunky young rider named Freddy Dixon, having his first Brooklands race ever. His Harley-Davidson was distinguished by the footboards he preferred to rests, and by the self-devised steering damper, the first ever seen on a motorbike in England. A third innovation by the ingenious Fred didn't work so well. Finding in practice that he continually slid back off the saddle, he glued on some emery cloth for the race. First it wore through his breeches, then through his underpants, and finally it started on Fred himself! As he later said, 'Was my .... red!'

was thrown off. He turned three somersaults, picked himself up, reputedly uttering terrible oaths, and tottered along to his fallen bike, remounted, rode slowly round to the pits for a new tyre, and went back into the race. Tough was Fred!

The running fight between Indian and Harley raged on, Le Vack heading Davidson until he stopped for plugs; Davidson then took over once more, leading at 300 miles at 72.25mph until, on lap 122, his luck failed and a valve broke. He tried pushing in, but with a shoulder weakened by machine gun wounds sustained in the First World War he ill-advisedly accepted outside help and was disqualified. That left Le Vack sitting comparatively comfortably, while behind the mechanical toll continued.

A Blackburne broke its crankshaft; the forks on Emerson's Douglas broke; Jack Watson-Bourne's Rex cracked its cylinder; S. E. Longman's flat-twin spring frame Wooler had dire mechanical ills; and O.M. Baldwin's Indian broke its frame. Five bikes – a Harley, New Imperial, Massey-Arran, Hobart and Acme Junior – went out with piston troubles, while A. Milner's game little 250cc 2-stroke belt-drive Levis broke its seat tube but continued after jury repairs. Lunchtime was coming up and spectators adjourned for picnics, but for riders it was a snatched sandwich and a hasty drink during routine pit stops, often with the new-fangled cine-camera-film men recording the scene.

Re-seated more comfortably, he sped back into the race, and when Davidson stopped for another tyre, "rooky" Dixon found himself leading the race at the 200 miles mark. But on his 82nd lap his front tyre deflated and came off along the Railway Straight; the Harley went down, skidding almost the whole length of the straight while its rider

Flat out or nothing. Drama attended the BMCRC's October 1920 meeting at Brooklands, when scratchman Reuben Harveyson (left), on the American Gene Walker's 130.43mph world-record-breaking eight-valve, 997cc single-speed, chain-drive Indian, made a tremendous effort to catch the race leader in the finishing straight. Having no brakes or hand throttle, he tore across the finish line, taking second place, then shot up and over the Members' banking, soaring into the woods. On his arrival at the paddock his only injuries, remarkably, proved to be a dislocated shoulder and torn leg muscles. Kaye Don (right), who started racing motorcycles in 1912, was famous for his exploits with the Wolseley Viper, works Sunbeam cars and Bugatti. Don broke the speed record on water in 1930.

'Call it PUR-JO' said the Peugeot car advertisements in the twenties. This is one of a team of vertical twin ohc 500cc Peugeot racing motorcycles built by the same great company. After several successes, peaking in 1923 with 23 victories, Peugeot's dominance gradually waned. The rider illustrated is Peugeot's No.1, Paul Péan, who retired from the 1924 French G.P. Three other Peugeots finished 3-4-5 behind British machines.

Le Vack's big red 998cc Indian was now a comfortable 12 minutes ahead of Dixon's Harley, and was lapping with metronome regularity. Officials studied their charts and watches, and just before 2p.m. began moving down to the finish line with the flag. Then, sensation, Le Vack was missing. Third man Reuben Harveyson came by on his Indian giving a vague signal, and Le Vack's anxious pit staff sent off a combination with a spare wheel by the inner road to the aerodrome in hopes of finding him. It looked as if Dixon might yet win, but then after three long minutes there came the familiar thudding exhaust, and Le Vack's Indian went past at speed. He had oiled a plug, and after changing it lingered for a smoke over on the Byfleet side of the track!

He completed the 500 miles in 7hrs 5mins 59.6 secs at an average of 70.42mph, still 9½ minutes ahead of Freddy Dixon's Harley-Davidson, with Harveyson (Indian) third, making it America 1-2-3. Fourth home, first of the 500s, and first British bike, was Vic Horsman's side-valve Norton, averaging 62.31 mph, and next home was rider/designer Cyril

Douglas brochure, 1927. The Douglas Engineering Co. was founded by William and Edward Douglas in 1882 and was a major manufacturer of motorbikes until the fifties.

Pullin on an ohv Anzani-engined Zenith with belt-drive Gradua gear. Half a dozen more big "1,000's" followed in, and 12th-and 1st in the 750cc class-came a flat-twin Coventry-Victor ridden by E.W. Parham, followed by W.H. Bashall's Martynsyde.

A big surprise was the 350cc winner, N. Norris's very standard 2-stroke single cylinder Ivy, which beat all the 4-strokes in the class. The 250cc class fell to Bert Kershaw's side-valve New Imperial, followed by Milner's broken-framed Levis, while local boys made good when the three Woking-built Martinsydes (two 750cc class twins and a 500cc single) won the team prize. In all there were 32 finishers – 50percent of the field – last of all being a Wooler, although a few other bikes struggled on until flagged off at the 12th hour.

Although Herbert Le Vack managed a radiant winner's smile, most of the riders were thoroughly exhausted from the physical battering, from long crouching in one position, and from noise, and the general verdict was "Stiffer than the TT". Even so, "Carbon" of *Motor-Cycling* enthused, saying "The 500

Racing in the rough: A.H. Alexander on his 494cc flat-twin Douglas raises a dust cloud on the very rough Le Mans circuit while leading the first post-war French Grand Prix, held in August 1920. He was very unlucky to lose all gears bar top, stalling at a corner and being disqualified for receiving assistance in re-starting.

Bert Le Vack, brilliant engineer and master rider, with his 996cc Zenith, built to his own specification.

Miles Race at Brooklands was brim-full of interest, and I don't think there is much doubt but we shall find it established as an annual event ranking only second in importance, perhaps, to the TT."

But it was not to be. Silencers were not, of course, in use then at the track, and many local residents were affronted at almost a whole Saturday's continuous noise from numerous rorty singles and twins circulating en masse. They lodged so vehement a protest that the BMCRC was not permitted to repeat their enterprising 500 Miles race in subsequent years: some manufacturers and riders were not perhaps too sorry, but it was a great race lost.

NEW ITALIAN TRACK
"The Motor Cycle" 1922

This week marks the opening of the new Monza 10 kilometre race track in Italy. The track has been built on absolutely up-to-date lines. It is situated in an erst-while royal park seven miles north of the city of Milan, and formerly belonged to the King of Italy, who gave it to the State. The track itself has been built in country consisting of agricultural land, vineyards and wood.

It is of peculiar form; one lozenge-shaped portion is described as a track, while the other is called a circuit, the two, however, forming one continuous speedway, with an under-ground passage, the circuit passing under the track while the grandstand will be outside, consequently the spectators therein will have in front of them a couple of parallel tracks with vehicles running over them in opposite directions. It is owing to this arrangement that the competitors will pass the grandstand three times per lap.

The track, together with the circuit, makes a distance of 10km. The width of the track is 30ft. in front of the stand, so that entrants may be started in groups.

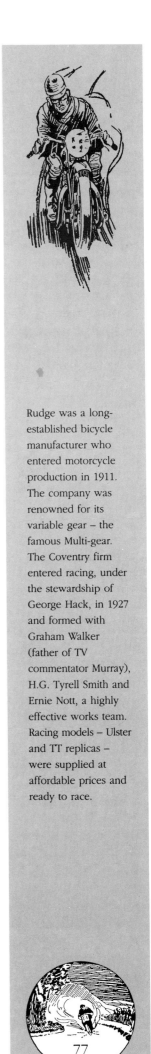

NUVOLARI
by Count Johnny Lurani

Nuvolari's early motorcycle races passed unnoticed, lost in the fog of brief summaries and hurried and inaccurate reports, especially as at that time he had not reached the stage where he could claim the critics' attention. Those who followed the races and were not too intent on the stars and leaders fighting for victory, but found time to study the fortunes of those in the lower classifications, had already been impressed by the riding methods of this obscure centaur, who was more often in difficulties through the vagaries of his engine than through the track or the skill of his adversaries.

The small, slender rider, all nerves and spirit, had a set of idiosyncrasies all his own. He would leap onto his machine in the manner of a High School horse rider, and his thin arms, which even the thick jersey failed to fatten, would be extended to enable him to grip the handlebars (those high, wide handlebars shaped like ox horns) as one would grip a sword, with the difference that while such as Ruggeri, Opessi, Gnesa, Vailati, Winkler, Visioli, Faraglia and other Italian aces of the time showed the strain of bridling the fierce bucking and vibrating of the front forks, that obscure competitor, lost amongst the also-rans, rode his machine as if it were a pedal cycle. Reports at the time were very skimpy and rarely spared a word for those who failed to gain glory, and were limited to a few words about the first two or three riders.

Thus it was that the early races of Nuvolari remained unsung and ignored at the Brescia Circuit in 1920 and in other races in succeeding years, and it was only in 1923 that the name Nuvolari appeared in motor-cycling periodicals, after his third place at the Rapallo Circuit (later to be known as the Tigullio). This track, which, even studied on the map, was enough to give anyone goose-pimples, suited the temperament of Nuvolari, or any rider capable of overcoming the lack of power and speed of their machines with personal courage and skill.

In March, then, the circuit of Rapallo was to see Nuvolari's first success as a rider, and he celebrated it in the saddle of a Fongri, the engine of which used two longitudinal, horizontally opposed cylinders and a magneto larger than the cylinders. Built in Turin, it enjoyed a good reputation for its touring qualities, but as far as racing was concerned could be likened to a draught horse in the company of thoroughbreds. It was a long machine with a rococo-style frame, all interlaced and curved. It was on such a machine, and such an infernal track, that Nuvolari succeeded for the first time in attracting the attention of both the spectators and the critics.

After a gruelling race of 155 miles on tortuous, hilly roads, Nuvolari succeeded in taking third place behind Piero Opessi on a Triumph and Enrico Manetti on a Frera, both overhead-valve, single-cylinder machines. The winner's average speed of 35mph. suffices to give an idea of the difficulty of the track; also the fact that only ten out of fifteen completed the course, and those who fin-

Advertising for Triumph from the inter-war period. The beginning of the thirties saw a new look in motorcycle design. The saddle tank and other innovations of the previous decade had come to stay, along with more shapely mudguards.

Top-line Italian ace Achille Varzi (left), son of a wealthy textile manufacturer from Galiate, near Milan. When he took up motorcycling he was able to afford the best machines, starting with Garelli and then going on to Sunbeam.

ished were widely separated. This third place earned Nuvolari an honourable mention in the foremost motorcycling publication of the time, in the following terms: "A Fongri ridden by an audacious young man created a good impression." The audacious young man was Nuvolari, and this mention, even though impersonal, served to break the ice.

A month later, Nuvolari was once again mentioned as being placed third in the 350cc class of the hill-climb from Parma to Poggio di Barceto, a classic of the time. Tazio had abandoned the Fongri and procured a Garelli. This famous and technically interesting machine used a two-stroke twin-cylinder engine endowed with great speed and power, but had the drawback of consuming large quantities of fuel and burning out sparking plugs by the dozen, which, however, was not to prevent him from reaping laurels and relegating in classification the riders

of the famous A.J.S. four-stroke, which was unbeatable in any race in which the Garelli did not appear.

The day of glory could not be far delayed. That day came in May 1923 on the Circuit of Parma, a fast, flat course with long straight stretches, but with a field of capable riders including Angelo Varzi, brother of the great Achille. Having by now got the feel of his Garelli, Nuvolari swept the board and won his first motorcycle race.

1930

PH

B·S·A Motor Cycling Annual

Sept 1934 or 1935

BSA Annual cover, 1921. Birmingham Small Arms never competed officially in races but were responsible for sporting singles. The 'Gold Star' BSA model, fast and reliable, modestly priced and of simple design, was a popular choice among clubmen.

Tazio had gained a certain amount of popularity in the motorcycling world before his first victory, for, in addition to his peculiar style of riding, he stood out from the other riders on account of his queer clothing, no less personal than his riding style. He would wear a heavy jersey with leather elbow pads laced on, over which he would have a sleeveless waterproof overall of that canary shade that was later to become his favourite racing colour.

In order to satisfy the Garelli's notorious hunger for sparking-plugs, he wore round his waist a "cartridge-belt" full of them. Later on, after he had experienced a broken chain, he wore a spare one, bandolier style, and when the circuit was a tortuous one he would add a pair of knee pads to his outfit. With those thin legs clad in knee breeches and soldier's grey-green puttees, he was the strangest and most characteristic figure in the Italian motorcycling world, in direct contrast to the propri-

Tazio Nuvolari (right)
with speed king Kaye
Don (left).
Originally from a
landowning family,
Nuvolari was born in
Casteldario, near
Mantua. He joined his
uncle, formerly a
famous racing cyclist
who had set up a
motor agency for
Bianchi, and started
racing motorcycles in
1920. A real
individualist, he went
on to win countless
car races and was
known as 'Il
Mantovanto Volante'
('The Flying Mantuan').

ety and refined elegance of Achille Varzi.

Class victories were no longer sufficient for Nuvolari's ambition. He meant to be champion of champions with the fastest speed in all classes. In view of this it was obvious that a 350cc machine would not do, so he entered the 500cc class, choosing from the various Italian and foreign machines a side-valve Norton, because Norton was the direct rival of Varzi's Sunbeam.

It was a prelude to the direct rivalry with Varzi, which was later to assume an almost epic aspect. But Varzi, certainly not intentionally, had at the same time chosen the Garelli 350cc so that the first big meeting between the two was postponed, for they were still engaged in different categories. Their meeting should have been on the circuit of Busto Arsizio in June, 1923, but though Nuvolari finished absolute victor on his 500cc Norton, Varzi came first in the 350cc class with the Garelli.

Even the 500cc did not suffice to satisfy Tazio's aspirations. There were other machines even faster, such as the 1,000cc American Indian and Harley-Davidson, with their ponderous, imposing vee-twin engines. These machines had brought glory to a number of famous champions and, each time they appeared at a meeting, would draw excited cheers from the crowd. Thus did Nuvolari pass to the 1,000cc class and to the Indian, with which he won the Giro dell'Emilia.

His next victory at Piave, with its arduous alpine course in the Dolomites from

Falzarego to Pordoi and Rolle, was fully covered by the Press. This race, open to all classes, drew an entry of all the best riders and finest Italian and foreign machines. Chosen officially as a member of the Indian team, together with the Milanese Erminio Visioli and the Tuscan Sandrino Lanza, Nuvolari was not only one of the few able to cover the difficult course at the average speed laid down, but also did the fastest time over the flying mile, thus gaining one of his most surprising victories and qualifying as one of the aces.

Those were the final years of sporting supremacy for the heavy engines, which were being beaten more and more in races by the 500cc machines, especially those of British manufacture, such as the Sunbeam and Norton, which were to dominate the roads of Europe. In Italy the only machine to offer them serious opposition was the Frera, and then only in long-distance endurance races like the Milan-Naples, but never on the short courses on which speed was essential.

In 1924 the decadence of the large American machines in European motorcycle racing circles drew attention to the duel between Sunbeams and Nortons, with Triumphs challenging hard. In the 350cc class, however, the Garelli was still dominant, and its most serious challenger was the four stroke A.J.S. ridden by Ernesto Gnesa, a Swiss who had settle in Milan.

Rivalry between Nuvolari and Varzi was becoming even more acute during 1924. To the composed, cold style of Achille Varzi was opposed the Garibaldian ebullience of Nuvolari, creating opposing camps of followers which were to become even more divided later in motoring circles.

This rivalry, however, was only a distant one, for, either by chance or design, these two contestants for the top place rarely came up against each other. Even in those days there were meetings each Sunday where they could gather laurels without having to fight each other.

It was a year of alternating fortunes; days of sunny victories and days of black misfortune for Nuvolari, who only required three

Italy wins! An unexpected Latin invasion of France came with the 1922 French Grand Prix meeting, when the Italian Garelli team of twin 2-stroke 350s won the class in the order Visioli (shown here), Gnesa and Dall 'Oglio.

The original Marston Sunbeam motorcycles, built until the late 1920s, were regarded as having the best workmanship and finish of all singles made in England. The factory, at Wolverhampton, was acquired by ICI, sold to Associated Motorcycles in 1937 and sold again to the BSA group.

SUNBEAM

Iotor Cycles

1938

VELOCETTE

For learner and expert

84

victories to gain his first title of Champion of Italy. The three victories started with that at Belfiore on his own Mantuan territory, followed by that at the international Circuit of Cremona and finally, completing the series, the victory at Tortona. That same year Nuvolari confirmed his place as a long-distance rider by completing the course in the Tour of Italy, although not too well-placed in the general classification. He entered on a comparatively small 500cc single-cylinder Indian; his American machine with one cylinder blanked-off.

In the meantime Bianchi had constructed a new machine which, with its original technical conceptions, compared favourably with those produced by other countries. It was a single-cylinder, twin-port, overhead-camshaft 350cc machine, capable of speeds that could upset the supremacy of the English industry, which in addition to the A.J.S. was now producing the Velocette, a motor-cycle which in spite of its different design was to take the place of the two-stroke Garelli.

The Bianchi, however, needed a rider capable of taking full advantage of its superb qualities – a rider who was equally at home on the fast flat circuits or on the mountainous courses.

The choice fell upon Nuvolari, especially as Varzi was fully engaged for the Sunbeam colours and no other rider had better claims.

Partly due to the happy choice and partly to Nuvolari's triumphs with the 350cc Bianchi, the sporting Press of 1925 acclaimed that year as the beginning of the golden era in the Mantuan's motorcycling career, a career which was to give a big boost to the Italian industry's efforts.

This famous "Blue Arrow" Bianchi had already made its debut, with Nuvolari up, in about the middle of 1924 on the Lario Circuit, which on account of its very tortuous course had earned for itself the title of the Italian Tourist Trophy. In that same year Achille Varzi was the first Italian to try the fascinating venture of riding for the first time in the Tourist Trophy, the oldest and most difficult motorcycle race in the world. He went to the Isle of Man with an Italian journalist who had

Opposite: Velocette, successor to Ormonde, VMC and Veloce, was headed by Percy and Eugene Goodman. Under Harold Willis, who raced and developed Velocettes, the KTT (a racing replica of the works' own grand prix model) and other ohc versions won in the Isle of Man TT, broke records at Brooklands and gained on the Continent a reputation for reliability and speed.

Famous contemporaries: maestro Tazio Nuvolari (wearing laurels) flanked by Achille Varzi (left) and Giuseppe Campari (right), Ulster TT, 1930. As motorcycle stars of the same period, Varzi and Nuvolari were frequently billed as principal adversaries. In reality they seldom came up against each other on the track, and started racing motor cars in partnership for the Bugatti stable.

Motor Cycling and *The Motor Cycle*, rival magazines, brought weekly thrills within the reach of the man in the street.

arranged a mount for him. This machine was the modest Dot, with one of those curious overhead-valve, single cylinder Bradshaw engines, the cylinder body having an oil cooling jacket while the cylinder head was provided with the usual cooling fins. A robust motor, fairly fast, but not in the same class as the Blackburne, J.A.P., A.J.S., Velocette or Sunbeam.

Although unable to put in much practice on the spot, suffering from the depression that seems to hit Italians when they ride in their first T.T., and his machine not one of the best, Varzi was able to merit words of praise from the severe English critics. Unfortunately, when in a leading position he was compelled to brake hard and swerve into the grass verge of the road, taking a bad fall, in order to avoid another competitor who had fallen in front of him. This gesture gained him the Nisbet Trophy, which is presented to a competitor for a brave and sporting action.

On the Sunday following the unfortunate expedition to the T.T., the Lario race or Italian Tourist Trophy was taking place in Italy. Varzi, knowing that Nuvolari would be competing with the new Bianchi, made haste to return to Italy in time, in spite of the fact that his knee was painful as a result of his fall. He was able to compete at Lario on the 500cc Sunbeam, but was forced to retire with engine trouble.

His brother Angelo was destined to have his revenge instead on his 350cc Sunbeam, in the race that was to mark the promising but unfortunate debut of the new Nuvolari-Bianchi combination. The 350cc class was won by Angelo Varzi whilst Nuvolari had to retire, though not before giving a demonstration of his capabilities.

It was in 1925 that the promise the combination had shown materialized with a series of successes. After winning easily at Monte Mario in Rome, and at the circuit of Padua, Nuvolari came back to the terrible circuit of Lario, with all the danger arising from its tortuous, killing course.

The Bianchi team, consisting of Edoardo Self, Valerio Riva and Miro Maffei, was cap-tained by Nuvolari. The opposition was formidable, but nothing could compete with the skill and technical superiority of Nuvolari and Bianchi, a pair who were to triumph after a hotly contested, gruelling race. It was an epoch-making victory, for which Italian journalists scoured the dictionary in search of new adjectives. That memorable win was reported thus by the most authoritative racing periodical:

"Nuvolari rode a marvellous race. He started determined to beat every record, but while coming down from Ghisallo his sparking-plug gave out, compelling him to freewheel to the pits, where he spent two minutes in changing it. Ghersi and Raggi, who were close on his heels, were able to shoot ahead. However, throwing himself with extreme temerity down the hill towards Onno, he was able to catch Raggi and to chase Mario Ghersi, who was going full out. At the fifth lap he was able to pass him and take the lead, which he held until the end. A heroic test, worthy of being told by poets capable of composing the most sublime hymns, and not by modest chroniclers like ourselves. Without the sparking-plug contretemps, Tazio Nuvolari would have been able to emerge absolute victor – and at Lario an absolute victory by a 350cc would have come as a surprise – and Tazio Nuvolari, as we were saying, has emerged with new, shining laurels added to his tricoloured jersey, which he won himself last year and which once again today he has proved himself well worthy of wearing."

Nuvolari's triumph at Lario was to be followed in the same year by his first victory in the Grand Prix des Nations at Monza, a most dramatic race marred at the end by rain. Nuvolari was alone with his Bianchi against a formidable array of British machines and riders, all famous men. Simpson, Handley and Longman were there, while the Italians, Angelo Varzi and Ernesto Gnesa, were also riding under British colours.

The 350cc and 500cc machines raced simultaneously, and early in the race Nuvolari, with fearless audacity, was able to

87

close up to the leading group of 500cc machines, from which point of vantage he was able to follow the moves of his rivals. Handley, winner of the Tourist Trophy, on a Rex Acme Blackburne, had succeeded in forging ahead, so that haifway through the race an exciting Anglo-Italian duel was taking place, as Nuvolari had been alone in passing Longman and Simpson. After various complications due to refuelling and plug-changing, it was only on the last lap that Nuvolari was able to beat Handley.

His four victories the year before became seven in 1926, including the memorable races at Lario and the Grand Prix des Nations, thus gaining him his second tricoloured jersey as Champion of Italy.

After Varzi's unfortunate initial attempt in the Tourist Trophy, repeated the following year with no better results, the Italian industry decided to make a mass assault against the apparently impregnable bastion of British domination.

The expedition had the full backing of authority, and a strong contingent with Pietro Ghersi, Arcangeli and Ugo Prini from Moto-Guzzi, Erminio Visioli from Garelli, and with Nuvolari, Mario Ghersi and Miro Maffei on Bianchis, left for the Isle of Man.

The climate of the rainy island, the correct but rather cold English manner, followed by the practice, always alien to Italians, of training in the early hours of the morning succeeded by long days of inertia, served as usual to shake the riders' morale.

The severe practice runs, rendered even more dangerous by banks of mist on the mountain section, were far from comforting for the expedition, especially for the riders who were facing these difficulties for the first time. Ugo Prini, who was reputed to be thick-skinned, was so demoralized that he begged to be allowed to return home. Erminio Visioli, who like Prini, was anything but timid, was all for retiring after the first lap. With the exception of Pietro Ghersi and Varzi, who – for Italians – were almost veterans of the T.T., all the beginners were nursing ideas about retirement.

All, that is, except Nuvolari, who seemed completely at his ease and who had caused astonishment during practice. In a practice spill, frequent on this diabolical course, he had fractured the small finger of his right hand, a matter of no account to a type like Tazio, who seemed impervious to physical

Achille Varzi, his racing as spirited as ever, on a Sunbeam in the 1930 Junior TT. The young Varzi sold his racing motorcycles to buy a supercharged, straight-eight P2 Alfa Romeo, an immensely successful racing car designed by the brilliant engineer Vittorio Jano.

pain, and he had continued training with his hand partially bandaged.

This bandage, however, did not escape the eyes of the racing officials who, upon learning the reason for it, ordered him to report for a medical examination which resulted in a categorical refusal to let him participate in the race. Nuvolari, not wishing to submit to this decision, turned up next morning at practice without a bandage on his hand, in the hope that the attentive officials might have forgotten the incident. Naturally he was forbidden to take a practice run and, in spite of all his protestations in Mantuan

Motosacoche (MAG).
Founded by Armand
and Henry Dufaux,
the Swiss company
retained Dougal
Marchant and Bert Le
Vack as their
designers. Marchant
produced, between
1927 and 1929, ohc
single-cylinder works
racing engines. Le
Vack devised the
superb 846cc sv V-
twin touring model –
his last design before
he was killed during
testing.

dialect, he had to resign himself to returning to Italy.

It went without saying that, even if his triumphs at Rome, Recanati, Riccione and Lodi had been fairly easy, his win in the Grand Prix des Nations had been hotly contested by the British machines.

Of his victory in the Grand Prix the periodical *Motociclismo* wrote: "Tazio Nuvolari, the audacious Mantuan, descendant of a line of heroic sportsmen, on Sunday roused the enthusiasm of the crowd with his victory on behalf of Italian motorcycling.

"Regardless of danger and counsels of caution, as is Ascari, this small, powerful bundle of muscle and will-power is a worthy successor to the calculated audacity of the 'Unforgettable', from whose district he has come in order to reach the highest ranks of the sport.

"Tazio Nuvolari is a man who has made himself, who wanted to make himself, reaching out with the active faith of the predestined beyond the limits of province and nation to the vaster horizons of merited glory in international motor-cycling.

"Neither the indifference of men nor the adversity of fate have been able to tire his dominating character, nor has he been poisoned by the seductive drug of ambition, repeated success or the impassioned enthusiasm of the crowd.

"Thus, enclosed in an impenetrable armour of youth and intrepid audacity, Tazio Nuvolari advances and conquers in the name of Italian motorcycling. May this fact assist him towards his goal and further victories."

RACING THROUGH THE CENTURY
by G.S. Davison

A fortnight after the 1924 Belgian Grand Prix came the French, this time held over the Circuit de Lyon. I had entered my 175 machine again, which turned out to be a mistake, for there was a big field in the 175 class and only one starter in the 250! The main thing that I remember about that race was that

the weather was extremely hot – so hot, indeed, that my Levis suffered from pre-ignition, as in the T.T.

Before the race I had fixed with Freddy Dixon to join him on the train to Paris and have an evening with him there – I wanted to study his technique in the Gay City. Unfortunately, the arrangement fell through; Fred had finished second in the Senior, whilst I had been third in the "175". The first three engines in each class had to be stripped for measurement, and the officials started on the Seniors; Fred caught the train, I missed it.

A few weeks later I met him and asked him what sort of time he had had in Paris.

"Oh, it was a bit dull" he said, "all on my own, except for one place I was in where they started fighting. It was a real 'do', with knives and all, and plenty of blood about."

"Did you stop them?" I asked, knowing his immense strength and force of character.

"Stop them!" he exclaimed indignantly. "Stop them ! No fear – it was good fun. When they began to quieten down a bit I just threw some empty bottles at them, to stir them up,

The redoubtable Freddy Dixon, hell-raiser, ace-tuner and first century-lapper at Brooklands with a sidecar.

Art and the motorcycle – pen-and-ink drawing by Nickless.

Wal Handley, winner of the 1930 Senior TT on a Rudge, with entrant Jim Whalley.

The Nürburg Ring at Adenau, in the Eifel Mountains, opened in 1927. The racing roadway centred around the village of Nürburg, with a medieval castle overlooking pits and paddock.

like. They were going at it properly when the 'gendarmes' came in. Stop them, indeed!"

I have always regretted that I had been unable to catch that train with Freddy; as it was, I never had another chance of an evening in Paris with him.

HUBERT HASSALL ON CONTINENTAL EVENTS
"Motor Cycling" 1924

"I have done a good deal of racing on the Continent, and in my time it was practically a certainly that the winner would be a British rider on a British machine. Things have

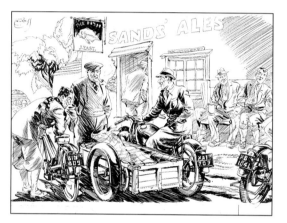

altered in the past year or two, however, and some of the French and Italian machines, notably the Peugeot and Guzzi, are terrifically fast. They will undoubtedly give our cracks a good run for their money, and it is possible that they will carry off some of the most important Continental events unless our men take things very seriously."

W.D. MARCHANT. THE FAMOUS SPEEDMAN
"Motor Cycling" 1926

It cannot be too greatly emphasized that any motorcyclist wishing to become a star professional racing man must be a first-class mechanic. If he has had a factory training all the better. He must be able to diagnose trouble at a moment's notice, for the secret of tuning is the rectification of one trouble after another. The man who is most successful in racing is he who is smartest at putting a finger on the restrictive factors.

The would-be speedman must be prepared for innumerable set-backs throughout his career. He must be connected with a manufacturing concern, or he is beaten at the start.

THE NÜRBERG RING OPENED
"The Motor Cycle" 1927

The Nürberg Ring, at Adenau, Germany, which is the largest racing "roadway" in that country, was opened on June 18th in the presence of representatives of the German government. It is by no means an ordinary racing track, nor is it a stretch of the public highway temporarily devoted to racing purposes. It is a racing roadway especially constructed for high-speed motor and motorcycle racing, and in its length of 29kms incorporates gradients and curves calculated to test the skill of the driver as well as the capabilities of the machine.

The roadway, which at no point throughout its length comes into contact with the public highway, is in the form of a gigantic figure eight, and is 27 feet wide. In the complete circuit are no fewer than 172 curves, of which 88 are left hand and 84 right hand. This means that in the course laid down for the motorcycle races (five times the complete circuit) over 850 curves have to be negotiated.

The track can be used in four different sections, as follows: the complete circuit, 29 km; the "Big Loop", 22km; and the "Small Loop", 7.6km; and by connecting up two straight tracks in front of the "Tribune", a track suitable for cycle races and motorcycle paced races is obtained. Eight different kinds of surface, including cement and tarmacadam, have been laid on this roadway and close observation is being made as to how each material stands the wear and tear.

A most efficient telephonic system of control has been installed, some ten main posts being scattered over the roadway; each has a

A big name on bikes was that of Dougal Marchant, tuner and rider, seen here on his very rapid 350cc Chater-Lea with Marchant-developed ohc conversion of a Blackburne engine. The bloated exhaust system, antecedent of the Brooklands 'can' (a form of silencer), was in response to the noise restrictions imposed at the track.

93

From wings to wheels. The 500cc model R23 production line photographed in 1923 at the old BMW aircraft engine works.

At the starting point an elaborate electrical progress board is installed, the figures being over three feet high. Sections of the crowd that have no clear view of this indicator are kept informed by loud speakers, while detailed information is printed on a special machine installed in the basement of the grandstand, and handed to Press representatives and others from time to time. A complete post office is to be found here giving direct telephonic communication with Cologne, Coblenz, Frankfurt and Berlin.

After the opening ceremony, the first event was racing for motorcycles.

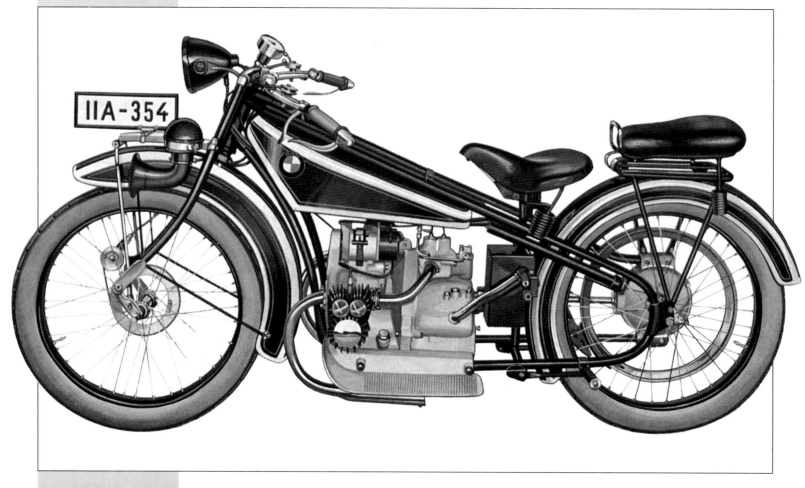

first-aid post attached. Between these main stations patrol posts are stationed, the officials carrying portable telephones, and as watertight contact boxes are to be found every 500 yards, they are in almost constant communication with the main stations.

There was only one serious mishap, which speaks well for the design of the roadway, for although difficult curves and turnings abound, careful banking minimises the danger.

94

RACING FEVER
by Hermann Lang

Now life could begin anew. For me, this meant a forthcoming race known as the "Solitude Race" – so-called after a hill near Stuttgart. The beautiful circuit comprised bends, curves and steep inclines through attractive woodland and round the old castle of Solitude. There was also a frightening hairpin, singularly tricky, since it was downhill.

Here we were in Cannstatt with an old machine; should we risk it ? After long deliberation, my brother lent me the cycle. What a

knew that my fellow competitors had better mounts, and faster ones. I had a maximum of 110kmh and at least 120 was needed to come anywhere near winning. None of that mattered to me. I was intent on grabbing at a chance, no matter how slender. I was going to race, even if it had to be on a broomstick.

A beautiful spring day was dawning as my brother and I set out to practice at Solitude. We arrived at the start and stood about rather nervously, somewhat overawed at the sight of the modern machines, accompanied by drivers of obvious experience. In spite of this, I mounted the machine and started the first

BMW R32. BMW maintained the basic design concept and developed faster machines, producing supercharged models for the works riders from 1928.

relief; my first motor race was really in sight. I was speechless and overwhelmed with joy !

I hadn't a bean to fit it out as a racing machine, but the foreman gave me permission to rebuild it in the workshop. Evening after evening saw me at work; it was hard. The dynamo had to be removed, narrower mudguards fitted, luggage carrier taken off. I fitted racing handlebars, polished the ports and manifolds, and after careful attention to the cylinder head, increased compression to take advantage of racing fuel.

My workmates used to pass by in the evenings and were doubtful about the old machine – they even worried about me. I well

practice run. The first lap went off well, and with renewed confidence I carried on for the second lap.

The ominous downhill hairpin had been overcome without difficulty the first time round and did not seem to present any obstacle on the second lap. "Seem" was right; I went in too fast and ran out of road ! Through pressing on too much I had cut out too late and landed rather romantically in a rose bush, from whence I rolled, less romantically down a fairly steep ditch. I was all right, but not so the machine. Front fork and handlebars were irreparably broken and spectators on the bend were highly amused!

Opposite bottom: BMW, R32. Founded in 1916 as an aircraft engine factory, BMW produced its first motorcycle in 1923. It was created by aircraft designer Max Friz and designated the R32. Unveiled in Paris in 1923 it proved the basis for one of the world's most prestigious and best-selling makes.

95

An assortment of
classic bike tanks
from the Golden
Years.

TANKS OF MODERN MOTOR CYCLES

CHARACTERISTIC COLOUR SCHEMES

This annoyed me beyond bounds, especially after noticing that my tail end was being somewhat overcooled by the spring breezes. Once more, a peculiar facility for tearing the rear of my trousers had shown itself. Whilst twisting myself round to inspect the damage, one of the policemen responsible for closing the road said, "It is idiotic to take this bend at such a high speed." Since I agreed with him, he became more human and helped me mend my trousers, behind the rose bush. Walking back to the pits, I felt really downcast and miserable.

How should I make my peace with my brother? By pretending something had gone wrong with the old machine? Oh, well – better make a clean breast of it! To my delight he was so pleased with my effort on the first lap that he hardly listened to my halting recital – he was not even annoyed.

What next? I simply had to be in this race. I was earning 30 marks a week then; 10 went to my mother and the remaining 20 had to cover all my needs, and since a month has four Sundays, one must have some fun, surely?

Without further reflection I decided – after all I was a mechanic – to mend my brother's motorcycle, damaged though it was. The owner of a nearby repair shop, whom I knew, was decent enough to present me with a second-hand fork, after having been told of my misfortune.

This miraculous gift came to me before the last two practice days, and there I was once more on the racing circuit of Solitude. I minded well the words of the policeman before entering the hairpin bend, and rode with considerable care. My practice times were reasonable, but no chance for a win, of course. So, Sunday and race day. I had terrible stage fright, and the other competitors had beautiful new machines. They had heard of my bad luck and looked at me pityingly. Heavens, yes, they were right. My machine was at least 5 or 6 years old; it had an old fuel tank, very little paint, and looked what it was—a second-hand old banger! Next to me on the grid was a competitor clad in

smart racing overalls, with a brand new twin-cylinder MAG.

Well, beauty is not everything, I said to myself; then came the start. I left the line determined that the hairpin should not cause me any difficulties. Only one rider was before me after the start, and I had to ride like mad to hold him. On the straight his machine was 10 kilometers faster, therefore I had to beat him on the bends – if I wanted to beat him at all. I managed to catch him up and overtook. Slowly it appeared as though I might win.

From then on, I rode with ever-increasing confidence. Then, 3 kilometers from the finish, I caught a tremendous clout in the back. Turning round furiously, I found the rear mudguard attachment broken. This demented mudguard slipped on to the rear wheel and was thrown up rhythmically, clouting my back each time. Thrashed thus by my mudguard, I crossed the finishing line the winner. The tyre was already showing the breaker strip, so that I would have had tyre trouble very shortly. My brother was crazy with joy – the incredible had happened – the old banger had won. Unbelievable !

GRAND PRIX d'EUROPE – ROME
by Ted Mellors

Throughout the winter, we tried this and that in the eternal search for more speed, and in April 1932 it was decided to enter a 350 in the first big race of the year, The Grand Prix d'Europe at Rome.

Its was just about this time that sterling had slumped so that the ultimate cost of the trip was colossal. Fortunately, however, we did not know what to expect, so I set off for Italy – with a bike and some tools.

I lingered for a day in Milan to call on our agent there, and took the night train to Rome. Having a natural desire to see the Eternal City, I deposited the bike and my bag in the station cloakroom and went exploring alone. It is essential to be on your own if you want to see anything of interest – once you meet "the local agent", it is motorcycles, motorcycles and more motorcycles. Only by

BMW R62. The R62 came into production in 1929 and was the first 733cc model from the Munich factory.

Ted Mellors on a New Imperial. The Birmingham-based factory gained a number of racing successes under Norman Downs.

99

exercising the greatest ingenuity can you avoid doing hundreds of miles at high speed for the benefit of prospective customers in the district.

I took a walk round the centre of Rome after a good bit more sight-seeing, I made the acquaintance of our agent and went with him to survey the course at Littorio.

The track was laid out round the flying field and was roughly of pear-shape formation, quite flat except at the apex where there is a high, vertical banking about 400 yards long. The total length of a lap was two miles only, and with nothing but grass in the centre it was possible to see the whole of it without obstruction. Training was interrupted at frequent intervals by the arrival and departure of airliners, and surveying these both inside and outside the hangers provided a pleasant diversion to rushing round the track in leathers under a very hot sun.

On Thursday, Frank Longman turned up with a 250 O.K. and Walter Handley with a Velocette. This made a pleasant little party, and things went nicely in the evenings, when the Italian riders showed us the brighter parts of the city.

During the training Walter's gearbox decided to run tight, which caused him a bit of work; but otherwise there was nothing of incident, and on Saturday morning I drained the oil tank and refilled it with fresh oil before handing in the machine to the officials. The race was this year the Grand Prix d'Europe and was to be watched by the King of Italy, so there was a good bit of ceremony attached to it, and a Royal Box was erected facing the pits.

On the Sunday morning, the 175s and 250s were the first to perform. Walter and I were in Frank's pit during this contest and were able to see three Guzzis roar round together, as if connected with a piece of string, like three performing monkeys, riding exactly to the signals from their pits.

The 350 class was next and there were about 15 of us on the line. We all got away so well that we arrived at the "Wall of Death" in a bunch. I was just about in the middle –

Velocette catalogue illustration, 1936. During the thirties constant improvements in engine efficiency took place. At the same time there was a general increase in weight due to the fitting of accessories.

and very uncomfortable it was, negotiating the banking in such close company.

After a couple of laps, Walter and I found ourselves in the lead. Our machines had almost exactly the same speed – neither was fast enough to get away from the other and though Walter went round the outside of me on the one corner where it was necessary to change down, in almost dirt-track style, I was able to re-pass him again as he engaged top gear. And so we sailed round and round for many laps until, on this particular corner, my bike went into an alarming slide. Reaching the straight without falling off, I soon discovered that the drain plug had fallen out of the oil tank and that the whole of the machine was well lubricated in consequence. (Thereafter drain plugs were always wired up!).

Walter lasted a little longer than I did, and then one of his overhead rockers broke so that we both joined Frank Longman and watched the rest of the race from the top of the pits. The event was won by the French Jonghi machine, which was destroyed soon afterwards in a fire at Montlhéry.

The 500 class was "the" race of the day, and was one of the best I have ever seen. The favourites, of course, were the three Guzzis, although they had been as consistent-

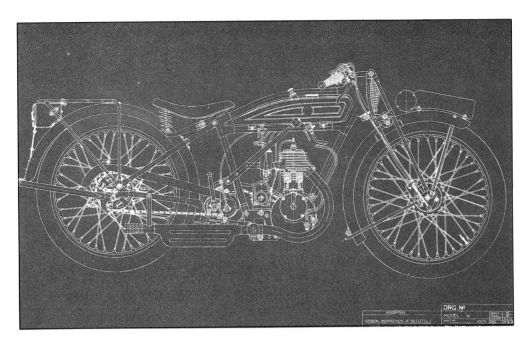

ly unsuccessful in the 500 class as they had been successful in the 250. The rest of the field was made up of private owners of Rudges, Nortons, Sunbeams, etc., and there seemed nothing to worry the Guzzis – or so we thought. In the early part of the race, indeed, the Guzzis were pre-eminent, but after one of them had gone through the straw bales (at the corner where I nearly did so myself), and another had come into the pits to make some adjustment, Taruffi, on a Norton, began to worry the leader. By superb riding, he gained a little each lap, and won the race, which seemed to please everybody.

THE VALUE OF GOOD PITWORK
by Ted Mellors

Pit work to the regular competitor becomes (with almost weekly practice) automatic, and the rider knows from signals how the race is going, almost as well as if he was a spectator himself. The time spent in refuelling is incredibly small, while the information imparted while he is at the pit is conversely just as large.

Road racing today is a highly specialised business. It is not picked up at one Grand Prix, or two, and although the machines and circuits are infinitely better than they were a few years ago, the dangers are much increased.

For example, the brakes of today are immensely more powerful than they were, so that one can approach corners at much higher speeds than before; but if a pin should come out, or a wire should break, there is little chance for the rider, in comparison with that of a few years ago, when brakes were poor, and were consequently not relied upon so much.

The same thing applies on wet days – for there is no control on the weather. Machines with ultra-powerful brakes are veritable death-traps, unless the brakes are used with the highest skill and discretion – particularly on the smooth tarmac roads that are often like skating rinks in the rain.

Constant participation in the Grands Prix, however, eliminates most of the guesswork in the preparation of the machines, so that with the previous year's data on the circuits, it is possible to be ready for the race soon after arrival at the location, though newcomers may require several days practice to be in the same position by race day.

How it all began: blueprint from the drawing office showing the general arrangement of a 277cc Triumph motorcycle.

Founded between the wars, Universal was a Swiss motorcycle
manufacturer whose machines were sold under the Helvetia name.

THE ENDLESS QUEST FOR SPEED

"Now! Now!" cried the Queen. "Faster! Faster!"

"*Alice Through the Looking Glass*" Lewis Carrol

MOTORCYCLING, MOTORING AND FLYING
by Hans Stuck and
E.E. Burggalten
"Motoring Sport" 1936

If I were to consider in a critical manner the three kinds of sport – Motorcycling, Motoring and Flying, I should say that motorcycling is the most sporting, motoring is the most dangerous, and flying the most enjoyable.

And there is the question which is often discussed: what is the point of making records? Are they simply just sporting affairs which happen largely through the ambition of their creators? Certainly they are. But they also have a great practical significance, since they show what is really attainable by continually pushing up the limit. And within this limit much can and must still be done.

We are only at the beginning of evolution. Thirty or forty years ago no one would have dreamt of these mean travelling speeds, and at the end of a like span of years from now similar progress will have been made, for which not alone the advance in design of the internal combustion engine will be responsible, but also improvement in road surfaces and other factors.

And now for the kernel of the matter: motoring sport is the driving force of development. There is this that distinguishes it from all forms of sport: it is a means to a end. It does not only serve an idea, it serves a great cause. Its practical value for the people as a whole is closely connected with sport. It is the product of an industry employing many hundred thousand men; it is of service to the whole nation; those who fell for it, sacrificed their lives in a great cause.

GUTHRIE, THE RACING "STAR"
The Motor Cycle 1935

How much more difficult it is – indeed, next to impossible – for the budding star of to-day to break down the barriers and get his chance as one of a "works" team. There are so few makes to be approached. Guthrie himself had

a hard enough task. Already he had done well in speed trials, sand events and hill-climbs. True it was in a small way, but he had been racing on his own account for five years and more. He started in 1920, following a spell in the Army as a Despatch Rider, and he had ridden in the Island in 1923 on a Matchless, more or less as a private owner.

Having regard to his speed trial successes it might have been thought that some manufacturer would have sat up and taken notice of his possibilities as a racing man, particularly in view of the hold racing had upon the public. The way he got his chance is interesting. He was always a clever mechanic, and he succeeded in tuning his A.J.S. until it was moving really well. It was the Druridge Bay speed trials in 1926 that set him on the path to fame. Bert Le Vack, Brooklands idol and one of the most famous racing men of the day, was there; so was another well-known New Hudson rider, Ted Mundey, while looking on was Price, who was the managing director of the New Hudson company.

Guthrie had already approached Price but without avail. The private owner proceeded to wipe up Le Vack, winning both the 350c.c. and 500c.c. events, a lone man with no works' backing against a powerful company and two of the best-known men in the racing world....

Along rushed Price and asked Jim whether he would ride for New Hudsons. Jimmy would and did. "Things went very smoothly after that," says Jim.

The following year he made his first pukka appearance in the Isle of Man, and if you look up the records of past races you will find J. Guthrie (New Hudson) second in the Senior of 1927. He was a made man, and I believe I am correct in saying that from that day to this Jimmy Guthrie has only once finished a race without being either second or first. How many races this means in all goodness knows. In 1935 alone he was first in the Junior T.T., second in the Senior T.T. – beaten by a mere four seconds – first in the 500c.c. North-West "200," first in the 500c.c. Swiss Grand Prix,

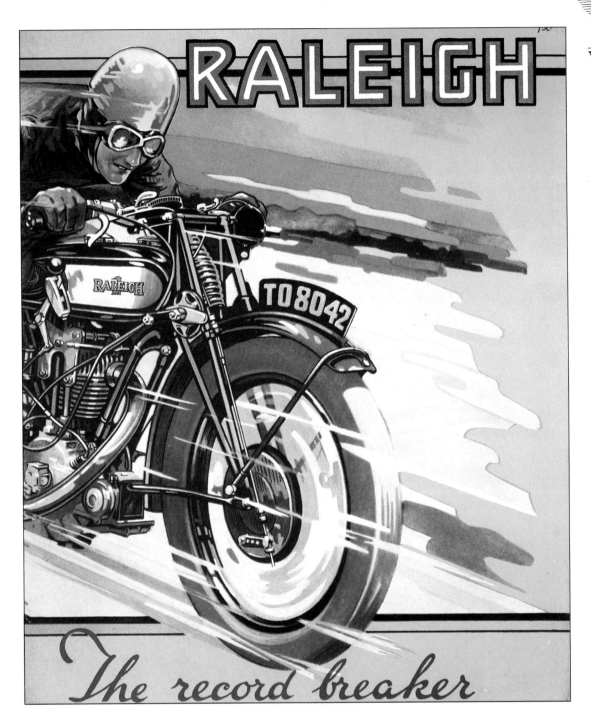

RALEIGH

The record breaker

Raleigh, 1930. The 1920s were the heyday for the Nottingham concern. As Chief Designer at Raleigh (Sturmey-Archer), tuning wizard D.R. O'Donovan, formerly Competition Manager for Norton and an ex-racing motorcyclist, devised some very quick ohv racing engines.

second to his team-mate, Rusk, in the 350c.c. Swiss Grand Prix, first in the 500c.c. Dutch T.T., first in the 500c.c. German Grand Prix, first in the 500c.c. Belgian Grand Prix, first in the 500c.c. Grand Prix of Europe (Ulster) at 90.98 m.p.h., first in the 350 and 500c.c. classes of the Spanish T.T., and, more recently, has raised the 500c.c. hour record – the "Classic Hour" – to 114.09 m.p.h.

No fewer than nine firsts and two second places in famous international road races in a single year—what a record ! And if you talk to Jimmy you will be told that he owes it all to Nortons: to the machines, to the directors, to Joe Craig, to the design staff and to the Norton mechanics.

MOTOR-CYCLE RACING
By James Guthrie
1934

Motor-cycle racing is not the foolhardy pastime that many would have us believe; The story of the racing motor-cycle is one of long experiment and research, careful test and gradual elimination. When I look round, as sometimes I do, with pride at the old collection of racing machines I have treasured, I wonder how in the name of all that is miraculous they ever stayed the course – for sometimes they did, although sometimes they didn't! The old riders achieved what they did with ill-designed frames, brakes that didn't, narrow tyres, transmission that just about transmitted and no more, gearboxes that insisted upon so delicate a touch – I stand in awe and amazement.

Road racing has been my own particular speciality, and perhaps the Tourist Trophy races held each year in the Isle of Man since 1907, except during the interval of the War, can be regarded as the Blue Riband of Motor-Cycle Road Racing events. In 1907, a Norton machine—a make to become famous in subsequent years, and to have to its credit more International Road Racing successes than any other—was successful, in winning at a speed of 36.2 m.p.h. There was no limit to the capacity of engines in those early days, machines with single cylinders were required to cover 90 miles at least, and the twins had to do 75 miles on one gallon of petrol. In the 1908 Tourist Trophy races the petrol allowance was reduced to 100 and 80 miles respectively. This event first became purely a race in 1909, when the question of petrol consumption was no longer considered; and it is interesting to observe that this was the first time that a pedalling gear was inadmissible. Time and time again the course has been changed and the rules either relaxed or tightened up. In 1914 a Rudge-Multi was successful in winning the Senior race at a speed of 49.5 m.p.h. In 1920, which saw the first post-War Tourist Trophy Race, a Sunbeam machine was successful in winning at a speed of 51.48 m.p.h. Gradually, from 1920, the speed increased – with the exception of 1928, when it was won at a speed of 62.98 m.p.h. – until in 1933, for the

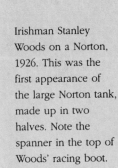

first time, an average speed in excess of 80 m.p.h. was achieved, the race being won by a Norton machine at 81.04 m.p.h.

Endless time and energy and a mint of money have been spent in research, not only in design, but in the investigation of materials. Most races are won or lost before the machines leave the works where they are produced. To find a few extra miles per hour in these days is not an easy task: from stem to stern all the details of the machine must be carefully considered, for not only is it necessary to have a fast and reliable engine, but all sorts of other factors enter into the matter. The surging power of the modern racing engine necessitates a gearbox that will stand the strain, brakes have to be right so that speed can be used with safety, and the

ILEY WOODS immediately after winning 1926 Senior T.T. on a Norton

Irishman Stanley Woods on a Norton, 1926. This was the first appearance of the large Norton tank, made up in two halves. Note the spanner in the top of Woods' racing boot.

107

Spanish TT races, Bilbao, 1935, with James Guthrie at the finish of the Senior race. Riding Nortons, Guthrie won on three successive occasions (1933-35) and in both classes (350cc and 500cc). Shown left to right are the Italian engineer Arturo Palmero, from the Ansaldo factory, J.G. Guthrie, Philbin, A.F. Nava and the French rider Naudon (Velocette).

108

steering propensities must be beyond reproach. It is, of course, a most important factor that the rider shall have confidence in his machine from the point of view of safety.

There are other aspects of motor-cycle racing, such as short distance sprint events, of which perhaps the best known is the hour record. In 1924 this was held by Victor Horsman, a pioneer from Liverpool – a born engineer as well as a racer -at a speed of 88.21 m.p.h. Today it is held by C.W.G.Lacey at a speed of 110.8 m.p.h. The World's speed record, 500 c.c., is held by a foreign machine at a speed of 139 m.p.h. This of course, was with a supercharged engine.

As a boy I knew all about the Tourist Trophy Races. In 1907 my father purchased a 3 h.p. N.S.U. – a German-made machine with low-tension magneto and tank controls. My first ride astride a motor cycle was taken without parental approval – whether the thrill of the ride or the anticipation of chastisement to follow was the greater I cannot remember!

In those early days, racing being permitted on the roads, hill climbs at speed drew me like a magnet, and whilst I had little expectation then of ever indulging in the thrilling sport, the time came when I became a competitor myself.

In 1914, like many others, clad in khaki, I was able to ride to my heart's content, and despatch-riding undoubtedly provided me with many thrills and an invaluable experience of which I have made as much use as possible in subsequent years. I have had many thrills in the various British and Continental events in which I have competed. The Isle of Man, where one rises at 4 a.m to take part in the official practising, and where one can cover 150 miles at 80 m.p.h. before breakfast, obviously embraces many. The roads are closed, it is true, but then no power on earth can stop a wandering sheep meandering over the road, or perhaps a few fowl from a highland homestead suddenly deciding they would like to cross the road. To

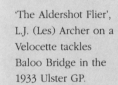

come round a bend at over 100 m.p.h. on two wheels and hit a sheep in the middle of the back is not an experience one looks for and enjoys, but this happened to me, and I am alive still to tell the tale.

Prior to the 1934 road racing season, I had made up my mind a long while ahead that I was tackling 1934 road races in real earnest. During the winter months of 1933-4 I rode almost every day for practice, sometimes on ice and snow in the Highlands of Scotland. I exercised my body methodically, practised breathing at high speeds with goggles pressed hard against the face; and I even went to the trouble of having an operation to help with my breathing. It is true that on the open road

one cannot approach T.T. conditions, owing to the many hazards, but skin which has become tender soon hardens. During one morning, for instance, I found that my glove had completely worn through where the thumb had been pressing against one of the controls. It had rubbed through to the bone and being numb I had not realised the depth of the injury.

In the 1934 Junior Tourist Trophy Race, which I was successful in winning at a record speed of 79.16 m.p.h., I had little or no thrills. Wet tar certainly gave me a spot of bother and made restraint desirable and even necessary at various points. The Senior race opened under very depressing conditions, the

'The Aldershot Flier', L.J. (Les) Archer on a Velocette tackles Baloo Bridge in the 1933 Ulster GP.

109

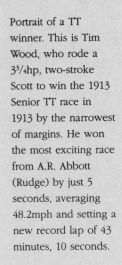

Portrait of a TT winner. This is Tim Wood, who rode a 3³/₄hp, two-stroke Scott to win the 1913 Senior TT race in 1913 by the narrowest of margins. He won the most exciting race from A.R. Abbott (Rudge) by just 5 seconds, averaging 48.2mph and setting a new record lap of 43 minutes, 10 seconds.

Claude Temple on a race-winning Harley-Davidson, 1921. A constant attraction in racing, Temple turned the world's first 100-in-the-hour at Montlhéry on a big-twin Anzani with main frame joints *soldered* together.

weather being bad owing to rain and mist on the mountains. I had looked forward for some days to some really fast motoring in this event – but restraint was my watchword; yet through the mountain fog I rode as fast as I possibly could, feeling all the time that valuable seconds were being lost. On certain parts of the course I opened up to full bore when visibility was but a few yards. I took my bearings in one case from a banner at the Creg, then counted three and braked, but this proved too early, and I nearly came off. The wet condition of the roads produced a tendency on many of the bends for the machine to slide, so that careful braking, careful gear-changing, and opening and closing of the throttle were necessary. This was very galling. Eighty m.p.h. was the maximum speed, and yet considerably more could have been achieved had weather conditions been different. In the mist on the mountains it was difficult to pass another competitor. Visibility was so bad that one would find a rider on the wrong side of the road near a grass verge, and would have to heel over to the other side to pass him.

Looking back briefly over my racing experience, if there is no single incident which stands out violently, there are many which have given me some real thrills, especially on the Continent. The spectators are often a source of concern to me, for they throng the banks and bends, and I have found It necessary on more than one occasion to cut very close on a corner to frighten them into a safer position, only to find on the next lap that they are back again in the old spot. Spectators, I think, often get more thrills than the actual rider when a machine has shown a vicious swerve, for instance, or taken some unexpected bend or dip.

Motor-cycle racing is full of thrills, and it is not void of romance either.

100 MILES IN THE HOUR
"The Motor Cycle"
1925

The study of motorcycle record history is of absorbing interest, since there are many incidents which stand out prominently among the mass of figures involved. "Milestones" in that history of progress include the first occasion on which a machine covered a mile in a minute, then of the first machine to cover 60 miles in the hour, the first machine to attain a speed of 100mph., the first to do two miles in under one minute and, lastly, the achievement

Archetypal trackcraftsman Albert Denly after completing one hundred miles in sixty minutes on a '500' Norton in 1927 at Montlhéry. His successes riding Nortons, first under Don O'Donovan and later under Nigel Spring, were legion and included countless world records in the 350cc and 500cc classes, both solo and sidecar.

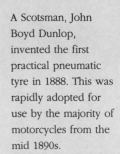

of the 1925 racing year which can now be recorded, of a motorcycle travelling over 100 miles in the hour for the first time.

This remarkable performance took place on the Montlhéry track on the 7th inst. In a no-trouble, non-stop, run C.F. Temple, mounted on a 996cc O.E.C. – Temple –

A Scotsman, John Boyd Dunlop, invented the first practical pneumatic tyre in 1888. This was rapidly adopted for use by the majority of motorcycles from the mid 1890s.

Anzani, covered 101.98 miles in the hour. He travelled 164km 117m in the hour, beating his previous performance, 160km 118m. These are world's records subject to confirmation.

The machine was built by the Osborn Engineering Co., of Gosport, specially for Temple. The equipment consisted of Hutchinson tyres, Shell oil and petrol, Lodge plugs, Coventry chains, Brooks saddle, Hartford shock absorbers, and a Contantinesco carburettor.

Temple made his arrangements well beforehand, ordered his tyres in advance, and bespoke a van to carry his machine from railway terminus to track. Unfortunately, in the meantime, according to the French Press, Temple had passed away. Like some of their British contemporaries, the French newspapers confused him with his ill-fated namsake, who lost his life while practising for the Amateur Road Race.

All arrangements were therefore cancelled, but to everyone's astonishment and delight, Temple turned up alive and well, but distinctly annoyed that nothing was ready for him. However, his French friends were immensely pleased to see him, and the manager of the

Montlhéry track was so thrilled with joy that he forthwith ordered two bottles of sparkling wine !

Temple, who is 30 years of age, has done some brilliant speed work since the war, first on a Harley-Davidson, then on a British Anzani, and since on various machines embodying his famous pressure balanced, overhead camshaft, British Anzani engine. In the last week of April, 1921, he, together with H. Le Vack (Indian), and D.H. Davidson (Harley-Davidson) was feverishly attacking the flying kilometre with a specially prepared Harley-Davidson from Milwaukee in an endeavour to raise the speed over the 100 mph. mark. He put up a time of 99.86mph, and seemed within an ace of making motorcycle history, but next day Davidson was the

Martin JAP, 1933. J.A. Prestwitch and Company was a fine, enterprising concern that built engines which powered innumerable British and foreign motorcycles. Hot JAP singles scored IOM TT victories in 1925 and 1927 (HRDs), 1928 (OK Supreme) and 1929 (Excelsior). In 1937 Eric Fernihough gained the absolute motorcycle speed record for Britain on his blown JAP-engined Brough.

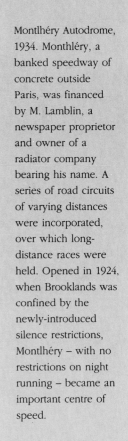
lucky one, and Temple, content that a Harley-Davidson had won the honour, made no further attempts.

In the past three years C.F. Temple has been a constant "attraction" at Brooklands, often experiencing the worst of luck, yet always a potential record breaker. Up till a month ago he held the record for the fastest short distance race on the Weybridge track, won at a speed of 109.9mph. Quite recently he got within a fraction of 1 mph. of averaging 100mph. for an hour at Montlhéry, but this time, unlike in 1921, he has himself taken his "just below" figure over the "century".

Temple has been extraordinarily fortunate in the matter of crashes. He has come off his machine at various speeds up to 90mph. on one or two occasions, but has never been seriously hurt. On the other hand, a crash in the Isle of Man in 1924, when he was practising for the Junior T.T., cost him a broken collar bone. Apart from this one instance, he has never been seriously injured, in spite of the almost continuous high speeds he indulges in on every appearance on the race track.

BROOKLANDS OR MONTLHÉRY?
by W.D. Marchant

Montlhéry is really no faster than Brooklands. On the score of comfort, both with riding and tuning up, however, there is no comparison between the two. Montlhéry has it every time.

RECORD BREAKING IN THE DARK
"The Motor Cycle" 1927

Each year one or more Norton machines undergo a strenuous certified test under A.C.U. observation. In these tests the one aim of the Norton manufacturers has always been to prove the capabilities of standard productions.

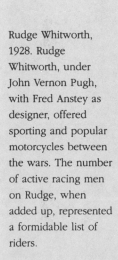

This year the test is, if anything, even more ambitious than usual. It started with the A.C.U. engineer, A. Prescott, taking at random from the Norton stores six standard 490cc. push-rod o.h.v. engines, complete with magnetos and carburettors. The engines were packed into cases and transported to Brooklands track. Then, after being fitted in a frame, each engine, without any preliminary warming in, was driven one lap (2.767 miles), whereupon it was timed over the flying kilometre. With the least powerful of the six engines the speed over the kilometre was slightly more than eighty miles an hour, and with the best engine it was 83mph.

Next A.V. Ebblewllite, of the A.C.U., selected one of the six engines by the simple expedient of drawing lots, and R.M.N. Spring, who is in charge of the Norton activities at Brooklands, chose one of the remainder by the same method. The latter engine was fitted in a frame with the object of making an attack on the double twelve-hour world's record. While the former was handed over to P. Pike for a long-distance road test under the observation of the A.C.U. engineer.

At 8 a.m. the attempt on the record began. Since the engine had not covered more than five miles, and was therefore far from run in, the first few laps were taken comparatively gently, the average speed being slightly under 60 mph. After allowing the engine to settle down a little, Spring, C. S. Staniland, and J. L. Emerson, riding alternately in two-hour shifts, lapped with monotonous regularity at a set speed of 64 to 66mph Shortly before dusk A. Denly, who was to be the "night bird", took over the machine, and four cars were brought into use to provide illumination. Three of the cars were stationed at various points on the track, but the fourth, a two litre Lagonda, followed Denly so that the latter might ride in the beams of two powerful head lamps.

Brooklands in the dark seemed almost uncanny; nothing broke the silence except the hum of the exhausts each time the car and the motorcycle passed the Fork. As a spectacle it was magnificent. The small knot of spectators gained an impression of speed

Rudge Whitworth, 1928. Rudge Whitworth, under John Vernon Pugh, with Fred Anstey as designer, offered sporting and popular motorcycles between the wars. The number of active racing men on Rudge, when added up, represented a formidable list of riders.

which no racing in the daylight can give. From the scoring box by the Vickers Shed's a little dot, slightly to the right of a blaze of light, could be seen as the Norton and the Lagonda passed from the Byfleet Banking to the Fork. Gradually the dot grew in size, and, with his helmet and leathers gleaming in the flood of light, Denly, with the car fifty yards behind, flashed by.

Unaccustomed to the track being used after dark, rabbits scampered about, and dazzled by the lights of the oncoming car, added a spice of danger to Denly's task.

Lapping steadily at 63 to 64mph, Denly brought the distance up to a total of 762 miles 1,438 yards by 8 p.m., the average speed for the first twelve hours being 63.57mph.

After being kept under lock and key overnight, the machine was handed over to the riders. The clearances between the rockers and valves were adjusted, and at 8 a.m., the test was resumed. All day long the Norton charged round the track, stopping only for petrol, oil, and a new rear tyre. At 7.13 p.m.,

the previous double twelve hour record in the 500cc, 750cc and 1,000cc classes was broken.

By 8 o'clock the total distance covered was 1,494 miles 1,216 yards, and so the average speed for the three new double twelve-hour records is 62.28mph.

Before the machine was locked up, the engine was partially dismantled for the purpose of checking its dimensions. In spite of the gruelling it had received it was in excellent condition: the piston and rings had bedded down perfectly, the carbon deposit was negligible, and the bearings had not the slightest trace of backlash. Only one fault could be discovered: the inner valve springs had fractured – a magnificent demonstration of high speed reliability.

ERNST HENNE, THE WORLD'S SPEEDIEST MOTOR CYCLIST

Having been racing for several years, it was my natural endeavour to become faster and

Germany's Ernst Henne (left), Heinneman (centre) and Britain's Eric Fernihough (right), 1936. Henne, who attempted to make the world speed record his exclusive property, used a series of BMWs for record breaking between 1929 and 1937

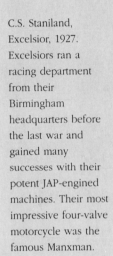

C.S. Staniland, Excelsior, 1927. Excelsiors ran a racing department from their Birmingham headquarters before the last war and gained many successes with their potent JAP-engined machines. Their most impressive four-valve motorcycle was the famous Manxman.

The holder of the spokeless chair wheel is R.M.N. Spring. Nigel Spring ran Norton interests at Brooklands from 1927, providing mounts for such riders as Bert Denly and L.P. Driscoll, before leaving in 1929 to follow a similar brief at AJS. Frequently, the fortunes of the day would turn on tyres.

119

Douglas, 1930.
Originally devoted to
the manufacture of
bootmaking
appliances, the
makers of the famous
horizontally-opposed
twin-cylinder motor-
cyles also produced a
sports car in the early
twenties.

faster, and that was how I came to be making
efforts to set up records. I had an opportunity
to follow up and study the whole procedure
of record attempts in Paris, and when B.M.W.
brought out a supercharged machine, I sought
to qualify for record runs with it. Much preliminary work had to be done, in order to satisfy the International Rules. In co-operation
with the A.D.A.C. of Munich I endeavoured to
find a racing track suitable for record-breaking runs, and succeeded finally in discovering
one close to Munich.

The first arrangements for such runs were
made by the A.D.A.C. (General German
Automobile Club). I broke the world's record
on the Ingolstadt Road on the 19th
September, 1929.

From that time onwards I have confined
myself solely to attempts on records, holding,
as I do, to the belief that it is better to
become proficient in one thing than to dabble
in several.

In the beginning these attempts to set up
records were fraught with great difficulties,
particularly in Germany where record breaking had not then been attempted on a very
large scale, although I am now conversant
with the most up-to-date methods and
arrangements.

So far as tracks are concerned, I am especially fond of the Avus, which I consider to be
the best track on the Continent, although it is
much to be regretted that this track is not eli-
gible for the kilometre international records,

Dunlop tyres for cars and motorcycles. One of the most important single developments in the thirties was the change from beaded-edge tyres to the wired-on type. Scientifically designed tread patterns notably improved roadholding and allowed motor-cycles to be ridden faster with greater safety.

Norton, 1935. The Birmingham firm, unquestionably one of the great names in the motorcycle industry, with an impressive reputation on the race track, produced their first overhead-valve singles in 1922 and won the 1924 TT with their design. The Model 18 made its debut at this time and it is of special interest that it remained in the Norton catalogue until 1954.

which is due to its having a gradient of 3 per cent, against a maximum allowable for this distance of 1 per cent. The shortest distance for which records can be run on this track is 5 kilometres. I regret it the more as the Avus to my mind would make an ideal track for 1 kilometre records. These are of such exceptional importance that it is to be hoped that the Avus track will be rebuilt to suit them.

HENNE DOES IT AGAIN
"The Motor Cycle" 1932

In the midst of the excitement of preparation for the big car race at the Avus Track, Berlin, Ernst Henne, the German speed wizard, went quietly out last Saturday and pushed up the 500cc and 1,000cc flying five kilometres to the extraordinary figure of nearly 136mph – the mean speed for two runs.

The Avus Track is wonderfully suited for record attempts of this nature, since it has two parallel and perfectly straight and practically level tracks, each about six miles in length. Also, the surface, consisting partly of tarred concrete and partly of ordinary concrete, is in excellent condition. Henne used the ordinary concrete part of the track, which has only recently been made.

He was on the spot as early as five o'clock in the morning, but he could not start before 6.30 a.m., as one of the timekeepers turned up so late. After doing a lap of the whole course to warm up the engine of his now quite old 750cc super-charged and streamlined B.M.W. flat-twin, he went to the start, and presently came shrieking up the course, crossing the timing strip at full speed. A few minutes later he came back on the return trip, and the new records were established for the five-kilometre stretch in both the 750cc and 1,000cc classes.

The records were held by Handley (F.N.) and the time stood at 1m. 33.4s., equivalent to a mean speed of 119.75mph. Henne required 1m. 22.8s, equivalent to the wonderful speed of 135.91mph.

RECORDS COURSE
"The Motor Cycle" 1934

Seekers after a course on which to attack the world's motorcycle maximum speed record are likely to be interested in a road which has just been completed near Gyon, in Hungary, and which, I learn, is available for such purposes. A long and gently curving approach (said to be safe for a solo at a speed of 100mph) leads on to a dead straight section of

three miles long, followed by another very slight curve.

Made of large concrete squares with bitumen-filled joints, the road is stated to have a billiard-table surface, to be almost without gradient, and to be nearly 20ft wide, while a 6 ft margin of hard, level earth on each side increases the safety factor.

The Budapest representative of the Vacuum Oil Company states that a record attempt can be arranged for a fee of £50 which includes time-keeping, telephone, road-closing etc.

RECORDS ABROAD
"The Motor Cycle" 1934

Ernst Henne, the famous German rider, and his equally famous super-charged 750cc B.M.W. machine, have made yet another successful attack on the world's maximum motor cycle speed records in both the solo and side-car classes. As a result the former has been raised to 152.93mph and the latter to 129.10mph.

The attempt was made on October 28th, on the new speed road at Gyon, Hungary

Numerous independent German companies started up in the aftermath of the First World War, only to disappear in the economic slump of the late twenties. One survivor was the Horex, founded in Bad Homburg by Fritz Kleemann, a well-known racing motorist, with his father, whose factory produced glassware under the Rex trademark. Using this name, and the first two letters from Homburg, the title Horex was devised. Hermann Reeth created, in 1932, ground-breaking 598cc and 796cc vertical twins with chain drive to the oh camshaft. The good looking racing Horex, of commendably advanced design, won many sporting events.

The endless quest for speed – C. Johnston (Douglas) passing the grandstand in the 1932 TT.

and, in addition to improving his own solo figures for the flying kilometre and flying mile, Henne bettered the sidecar figures over the same distances that were previously held by Alan Bruce (996 Brough Superior sc.). Henne then took out his 500cc B.M.W. and attacked the flying mile and kilometre records in Class C (500cc solo). He was unable to secure his kilometre record (held by Milhoux (F.N.) at 139.20mph), but he put up the mile figure to 137.26mph.

Henne's equipment included a Zoller supercharger and Vacuum oil.

180 M.P.H. ON A FIVE-HUNDRED!
Henne's Amazing Achievement on a Fully Enclosed and Streamlined B.M.W. 'The Motor Cycle' 1936

It sounds fantastic - 169.14 miles an hour on a 500cc motor cycle. But there was the cable. Eight world's records broken.

Many in the know were delighted, but not amazed. Had not Henne and his extraordinary-looking B.M.W. been seen on the Munich-Landengrenze autobahn on the previous Monday travelling faster than ever man had travelled on a motor cycle before? Yes, he was seen near Rosenheim at 6 o'clock in the morning with a completely streamlined 500cc transverse-twin B.M.W. A week or more previously Herr Sleischer, the B.M.W. team manager, had stated that they were finished with the 750cc model – the supercharged five-hundred was developing considerably more power than the old engine, although the latter was half as large again.

Yes, B.M.W.'s were ready, and with a completely enclosed, fully streamlined machine instead of the faired, semi-streamlined mount. The body, minus the lid, is very much after the style of a torpedo, and the rider is completely enclosed and looks through a small wind-screen. Handlebars – everything except the bottom of the wheels – come within the body.

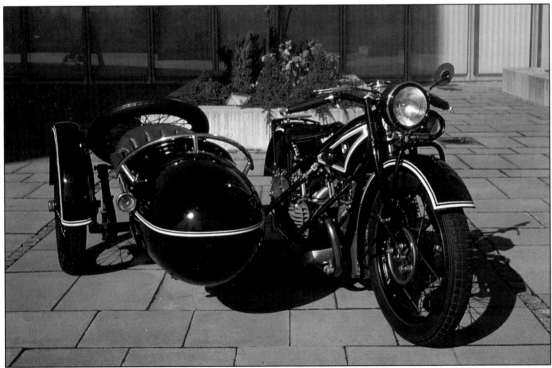

BMW R11. After the depression, the new regime in Germany encouraged the motorcyle industry by making available money for the development of advanced racing machinery.

BMW R52. German Steib sidecars found immediate popularity. Both BMW and Zundapp, to order, provided buyers of new models with a Steib attached.

125

What was to happen to the rider when he wished to stop? At each side a small wheel was fitted. When the rider was reaching a standstill he must let down this retractable undercarriage – if he remembered to do so.

Those in the know waited expectantly for the special little records meeting to be held on the Darmstadt-Frankfurt autobahn, which is, if possible, straighter than an arrow.

E.C. Fernihough was there by invitation with his supercharged Brough Superior. He had intended to attempt records in Belgium,

but was invited to join in at Frankfurt. He set the ball rolling by breaking Henne's standing start kilometre record in the 1,000cc class, raising it from 94.195mph to 98.91mph. A strong wind was affecting matters. In one direction he achieved 113mph-from a standing start! Later on he was to attempt the world's maximum speed record.

Henne took a hand. Those who had watched him practice at Rosenheim anticipated something verging upon the meteoric. Never even during the practising at

The 596cc Ariel, 1934. The celebrated ohc Square Four (the 'Squarriel'), designed by Edward Turner, first appeared in 1931. Chief designer for Ariel was Val Page, with Harold Perrey, a well-known rider, in charge of competitions.

Rosenheim had any vehicle appeared to them to travel so fast. Apparently the unofficial timing was – well, "unofficial"; nevertheless. Herr Sleischer, was secretly looking forward to a speed of approximately 180mph.

The amazing streamlined projectile, only about 2ft 8inches in maximum width, was to sweep past at a speed twenty miles an hour higher than that of the world's maximum motorcycle speed record. Less than 500cc and the machine covered the flying kilometre at 180.197mph. Again, however, the wind

entered into things. The mean speed was down to 169.14mph. Think of it, though, the world's maximum speed record raised from 159.10mph to 169.14mph - smashed by a machine of only 500cc and a one-way speed of over 180mph - an amazing, magnificent achievement of man and machine.

FERNIHOUGH DOES IT AGAIN!
"The Motor Cycle" 1936

Eric Fernihough returned last week to Budapest (where he recently raised the standing mile record to 108.24mph). This record – as in the case of the standing kilometre record which Fernihough holds at 98.91mph – was obtained with the semi-streamlined supercharged 996cc Brough Superior-J.A.P.

Owing to the difficulty of testing his machine properly before taking it on the Continent, Fernihough found that certain unexpected problems, which only became apparent at high speeds, prevented further record-braking runs for the time being. However, in the intervening period he overcame those troubles, and last Saturday took his Brough Superior over to Gyon, Hungary. There, over the flying mile, he averaged a mean speed of 163.82mph, thus beating by over a mile an hour Henne's speed of 162.7mph, which was made on the fully streamlined 500cc B.M.W. at Frankfurt.

Fernihough then proceeded to attack the standing mile sidecar record, which he did successfully at 80.49mph.

MOTOR CYCLE RACING -
PROSPECTS FOR 1937
by Max Prior
"Speed" 1937

So far as this country is concerned, a critical period has been reached in the history of motorcycle road racing; although for several years now it has been apparent that in at least one of the three classes for which road-race organizers cater, viz, the 250cc class, we no longer rank as undisputed "cock of the nations", not until last season did we appear

Brooklands timing clocks by Smiths.

in danger of relinquishing permanently our stranglehold on 500cc honours.

Now, however, it has to be admitted that Britain's fastest road-racing "five hundred", the Norton, is no longer Europe's fastest road-racing five-hundred. Speed, of course, is not everything by a long chalk in this particular sphere, and on the score of what may be termed race-worthiness, the Birmingham product still has a good season's lead on its nearest Continental challenger – by which of course, I mean the B.M.W.

The German supercharged flat twin created the sensation of 1936 by giving the Nortons a straight beating in the 500cc class of the Swedish Grand Prix. Alas there were no "ifs" or "buts" about it; both marques gave of their best – and the B.M.W's best proved to be the winning best. What the Norton gained on the corners and on stability during high-speed braking, the B.M.W. more than made up in sheer knots and dizzying acceleration

Up to a point, a machine possessing this quality of race-worthiness in an exceptional degree can afford a slight deficit in maximum mph. But we have seen what inevitably hap-

pens when that deficit grows beyond certain proportions.

The uninformed may reasonably ask: Why, if the Germans have proved the superiority of the supercharged multi over the unblown single, we do not take a leaf, or even a whole chapter, from their designer's book ? The answer to that is two-fold. Firstly, the motorcycle trade in Great Britain is at present enjoying a well-deserved revival of fortunes after a long period in (comparatively speaking) the doldrums. Those who have their money in motorcycle manufacturing concerns are naturally anxious to reap the full benefit of that revival, and the expenditure involved in the evolution of entirely new racing designs would naturally bite a fair-sized hole in these long-awaited profits.

Secondly, there is the widely accepted axiom that a road-racing bicycle, if its successes are to weigh at all with the prospective buyer, must conform – broadly, at least – to the standard product. In other words, while Nortons need not, and do not, make any secret of the fact that their T.T. jobs are built largely of expensive ultra-light materials,

Raleigh motorcycles were made up to 1906 and again after 1919. Raleigh, like BSA, Rudge, Triumph, Sun and Carlton, was ultimately absorbed by Tube Investments Ltd. These are famed marques which provided tangible evidence of Britain's one-time superiority in the industry.

it would not do for them to race, say, an in-line "four" unless they intended to put an approximately similar design on the market – and at a reasonable price !

There are, it is true, a certain limited number of motorcyclists who would fall over each other to possess a blown four-cylinder with the handling of the present "International" single and acceleration akin to that of a G.P. Auto Union. But the manufacturer cannot but be mindful of the thousands he has spent, over a period of twenty-five years and more, in telling the world, through direct advertising and by practical demonstration, that the good old single has the rest beaten for reliability and good honest guts. Though the day may come when he has to burn that cherished boat behind him, he is naturally reluctant to take the fateful step.

He knows there is no conservative like the die-hard motor cyclist; what was good enough for his father is good enough – with refinements such as enclosed chain transmission, big saddle tanks, fat-section tyres, etc – for him. There is, of course no reason to suppose that the unknown British single-cylinder

bicycle has reached the limit of its speed potentialities. For years now the pessimist has been gloomily foreshadowing the imminence of a full-stop to further development with this type of engine, yet, year after year, they have been confounded by the ever-growing prodigies of power produced by the good old single. The trouble now lies in the fact that it is no longer possible to go on finding extra horses fast enough.

The difficulty of supercharging a single successfully is well known, such designs as the flat twin B.M.W. and parallel-axis two stroke twin D.K.W. on the other hand, are admirably adapted to forced induction and so far from stagnation having been reached by these German marques there is reason to think that many more mph are waiting to be conjured up.

Apart from road racing, nothing like a proportionate value is placed by British manufacturers and accessory concerns on world records. It is so many seasons now since a British motorcycle was the world's fastest that one begins almost to despair of that distinction ever returning to these shores.

Nevertheless, while we have braves like Eric Fernihough with the spirit to sit a two wheeler at nearly three miles a minute; and brains like George Brough's to build machines which are not only rideable but safe at that enormous gait, there is yet hope. At the moment, the world's flying kilometre record stands to Ernst Henne and his "rennlimousin" B.M.W. at over 169mph. Fernihough, however, is not so very far behind, for he holds the mile on his Brough Superior at 163.82mph.

What next? Can either of these supermen go faster? As for Henne, his difficulty lies in holding on for dear life inside that "narrow cell" of his. Although the B.M.W. has an engine only half the size of the Broughs, it still had power in hand when it clocked that prodigious kilometer, but the slightest gust of wind made the bike practically uncontrollable. Dare Henne go faster ? That is the question.

Per contra, Fernihough vows that he had a

BSA catalogue illustration, 1931. The BSA marque was known primarily for singles of simple and inexpensive design.

Brough Superior, 1925. A sensational, large-capacity machine built regardless of cost by George Brough and promoted as the 'Rolls-Royce among motorcycles'. The fast Brough Superior set the standard for luxury and refinement. T.E. Lawrence – Lawrence of Arabia – was one of Brough's valued customers and owned seven SS100s.

comparative joy-ride at over 160.

Then, of course, there is Pietro Taruffi, who recently finished building an "egg" around his blown Italian four. He is all out to top the 200 mark.

Who first I wonder ?

STREAMLINING HAS COME TO STAY!
by "Ambleside"
"The Motor Cycle" November 1937

There is no doubt about it. Streamlining has come to stay for record-breaking machines. By streamlining, I do not mean a simple fairing-off of various protruding parts of a motorcycle. Modern speeds require scientific, aerodynamically sound, streamlined enclosure of both man and machine.

Last week I was fortunate to be present at the records meeting organised by the O.N.S. on the autobahn at Frankfurt-am-Main where time after time low, silvery shapes would roar past like strange projectiles in a world of things to come.

One moment they were a speck in the distance. Then, growing visually as their thundering exhaust notes rose to a crescendo, they would hurtle past at incredible velocities – so fast that the eye could scarcely follow – only to disappear down the long straight as quickly as they had come, leaving behind a faint odour of alcohol fuel and castor oil.

The O.N.S. is to be congratulated on its initiative in trying to shake off the general apathy that exists as regards records by introducing a competitive element. Invitations were previously sent out to likely record-breakers in other countries so as to add an international flavour to the week, and the Frankfurt-Darmstadt section of the Reichsautobahn was closed to all other traffic from 7 a.m. to 4 p.m. daily. All day long vast crowds thronged the bridges and sides of this

Swiss Grand Prix, 1938. Pictured is one of Germany's most famous riders, Walfried Winkler (DKW), who placed third in the 250cc race. Joerge Skafter Rasmussen, a Dane, founded the DKW company in 1919, and ten years on it became the largest motorcycle factory in the world. In 1932 DKW amalgamated with Audi, Horch and Wanderer – the quartet comprised Auto-Union. Chief designer of the very effective racing motorcycles was Hermann Weber, ably supported by August Prissip, chief of the competition department.

autobahn – proof of the interest the German public takes in record-breaking.

The section of the autobahn used for records up to ten miles is approached by a falling gradient of approximately three to four miles in length at each end. Then follows one straight of five miles and another of nearly four miles. The two straights and one approach are linked by quite sharp bends, that is, sharp when one considers the colossal speeds involved. For a greater part of the timed distances the autobahn runs in a cutting, but there are several open stretches.

The scientific adoption of streamlining was the outstanding feature of the meeting. The first machine to catch my eye was a two-fifty D.K.W – fully enclosed, of course – with a tail fin designed so that it could be split for use as an air-break. This machine also had a retractable "undercarriage". By pulling a lever, two arms with small wheels on their ends were extended so as to form two "prop stands", one on each side, for use when coming to a standstill.

The D.K.W. sidecar outfit was beautifully streamlined, and the "chair" was flared into the casing around the actual machine. With an exceptionally small and fully enclosed sidecar wheel it was difficult at first to believe that it was a sidecar outfit, but there was no doubt that its construction was in accordance with F.I.C.M. record-breaking regulations.

This was D.K.W.'s first attempt at serious streamlining, and because of this it will easily be understood that it was not quite so successful as at first hoped. To obtain a slight idea of the problems confronting the designer of such a shell, one should imagine that the streamlined machine acts as an aeroplane wing which is capable of producing a lift on both sides. In other words, as the motor cycle streaks down the road its sides are being subjected to a definite side pull or horizontal lift – that is, if it is of such a shape that the air in front is pulled back and along the sides.

As this pull is equalised on a theoretically correctly designed body it should not be noticed. But, owing to road shocks and side gusts, there is every possibility of the machine being pulled to one side, and this in turn would start wandering of a type that would be difficult to hold.

This in actual fact caused the D.K.W. riders to feel most unhappy at high speeds, so much so that on their smaller machines the shells were for the most part removed.

But now take a look at the B.M.W. machine, riding which Ernst Henne made several trial runs at high speed. This machine was remarkable for the fact that it held the road perfectly, and ran straight down the middle-line of the autobahn without a waver. It was really one of the most impressive pieces of high speed motorcycling that I have seen in years.

Why should Henne be able to do this and the other riders be troubled with wandering on machines whose steering prior to streamlining was unimpeachable? Henne's machine was designed by an expert in aerodynamics. The streamlining was tested in various attitudes in a wind-tunnel, during the course of which a vital point came to light. The air flow along the sides of the body was apt to flutter under certain conditions, while the flow on the other side would momentarily remain stable. Thus a side pull would be exerted.

To overcome this the tail of the machine – already fitted with a vertical fin top and bottom – was equipped with two vertical fins, one on each side which project outwards. Their object is, after the manner of flaps on certain aeroplanes, to pull the air back along the sides of the body by reason of their tendency to cause a vacuum as the machine hurtles down the road.

Admittedly, they must offer a certain amount of resistance to the air, but on the other hand they undoubtedly served their purpose in keeping the machine on a straight course.

Some I know will argue that such streamlining is dangerous, but properly designed and carried out it should, if anything, be safer, by reason of the fact that rider and machine can reach speeds of 200mph under aerodynamically sound conditions.

Complete streamlined enclosure of both

133

BMW, DKW and NSU, induced by the German government, shared in competition successes in an era when their supercharged racing machines were all-conquering.

Racing line – Eric Fernihough and Brough Superior on the Frankfurt Autobahn. British factory interest in 'world's fastest' honours was minimal and Fernihough's attempts were made as a privateer, with little support compared with Piero Taruffi (Italy) or Ernst Henne (Germany).

rider and machine requires an immense amount of study and prolonged wind tunnel tests. It costs money but is in the interests of design. Who knows that in fifteen years' time you and I will be riding machines like those I saw in Frankfurt last week?

170MPH - ON TWO WHEELS
A few days before his fatal crash – travelling at nearly three miles a minute on the Gyon road – Eric Fernihough prepared the following article.

A quarter of a century ago a very small boy, rummaging in the family wastepaper basket, found a catalogue of motorcycles and their accessories. He kept it, studied it, and from it learned to name the component parts of the machines he saw. It was dearer than any story book to him, for from it sprung a deep-rooted interest in motorcycles that filled his life.

Years afterwards he used to break bounds on Sundays and tramp miles from his school to an important road, where, for a brief half-hour, he could sit and watch various makes ascending a certain hill and compare their performances. A military aerodrome was another objective where internal combustion engines could be seen. Often he was late

back for roll-call, but that, to one who was obsessed with motorcycles as he was, did not seem important.

That small boy was I.

Those dreams have come true, and other ambitions besides I would not have dared to hope for in those far-off days. The Moon could hardly have seemed as unattainable as the motorcycle speed record did then.

My first bike was not a fast one. This was fortunate, for it is both absurd and dangerous for anyone to try to do high speeds without an enormous amount of practice on slower machines. When I tell you that the machine had been through the war, and flat out could be coaxed up to 32 miles an hour, you will realise that riding it did not involve any real danger.

A year later I got a Norton which would do 70 and after that one of the famous "90 bore" Zeniths, which carried me into the 80s. My first speed contest, a hill-climb in which I drove a Morgan three-wheeler, came about the same time, and resulted – nobody more surprised than myself – in an award for making the fastest car time of the day.

I went in for a lot of hill-climbs after that, driving the Morgan and also a 250cc New Imperial, but they were relatively small affairs. In the meantime, however, I had conceived a new ambition. I wanted a "Gold Star", to gain which it was necessary to lap Brooklands on a motorcycle at over 100 miles an hour.

A good many people had already done this on bigger machines, so l determined that I would get it on a 350 – a bike of two and three-quarter horse-power – and join the select minority.

The bike was prepared, and I went out. A lap or two to warm up and then full throttle. It seemed to be a pretty fast bit of lappery, and I waited anxiously for the time-keepers' figures. They came: 99 miles an hour! I went out again, with the same result. Time after time I lapped at over 99 without once touching the magic century. There seemed to be a jinx on that bike. But at last, after trying everything we knew to squeeze that extra scrap of power out of the engine, we got it. Nothing had ever given me so much satisfaction.

That was in 1933, and two years afterwards I built my first big "Twin". First time out the bike exceeded two miles a minute, and by the end of the season it had taken the Brooklands motorcycle lap record for all classes at 123.58 miles an hour.

This lap record was an achievement

beyond my wildest dreams. I had not even contemplated being able to do it when I was building the machine. Now, out of the blue, it had fallen into my lap, and my friends were trying to persuade me that I should go for the World's Fastest. I was a long time believing them, even though George Brough, maker of my famous Brough Superior machines, was sure we could do it.

Eventually, late in 1936, my first supercharged model appeared. Alas, it came too late. For in the meantime Ernst Henne, the German rider, had pushed the record we were aiming at higher still. Our best, 163.82 miles an hour, won the world's record for the mile, but could not top his figure for the flying kilometre.

You may think that record-breaking is all fun. Don't you believe it. For every second of record riding, I do a fortnight's work, and did I work that winter !

Strong-armed rider of big motorcycles: the experienced master, E.C. Fernihough was a serious contender for 'fastest in the world' honours. His record-breaking Brough carried a scalded black cat emblem on the front cowl (he was most superstitious). At Gyon in 1938, approaching an estimated 180mph, his machine – fully streamlined and sensitive to cross winds – left the road and he was killed instantly.

At the earliest possible opportunity in the spring of 1937, the moment the weather promised to be suitable, we loaded the machine on to my two-ton van and set out for Budapest, where the wonderful Gyon road, stretching dead straight for miles across the great Hungarian plain, provides a speedway it would be hard to equal.

But though the flatness of the plains is an inestimable advantage in one way, in another it is a disadvantage. There is always wind. We were forced to wait several days before it was calm enough for an attempt.

At last there was a lull, however, and I went up the road at 175 miles an hour, easily fast enough for the record. But a record, as you probably know, is worked out from the average speed of runs in opposite directions, and on the return run, with the bike moving once more at over 170, the enormous power of the engine sheared the key which held the sprocket. The sudden cessation of power

gave me an awkward moment, and made me realise the tremendous resistance of the wind at that speed, for the machine slowed just as if something had gone tight. Indeed, at first we suspected that that was what had happened.

It took us a couple of days to rectify matters, and then we went out again. The wind was still bad, and though we reached the road as usual at eight in the morning, it was tea-time before the breeze fell sufficiently for another run. Once again I made a good speed one way, only to run into minor trouble on the return trip.

We told ourselves that the third time would be lucky, and prepared to start again.

So for a third time I was pushed off. I settled myself along the tank, took a firmer grip, and gave her the gun. And this time nothing went wrong. By the time I returned, I had averaged 169.8 miles an hour for the two runs, and the record was ours.

But we had to curb our jubilation for a while; our job wasn't finished. For the next hour we worked feverishly fitting the sidecar to the bike and wondering, while we worked, whether the wind would hold off long enough for us to get the world's fastest sidecar record as well. Fortunately, it did.

With the sidecar attached I had a really hectic ride. I had to fight the machine all the way, and at one time I got the third wheel right off the road on to the grass verge. Since the bike was touching 145 when it happened, you may take it from me that was not one of life's pleasanter moments.

However, I kept on full throttle, and as I passed the timekeepers I saw on the "clock" that the machine was doing 147. The speed for the run was 143.5 miles an hour, which left us a comfortable margin over Henne's existing record, and we came back "quietly" at about 130, giving us this record, too, at 137mph average.

What is it like to be exposed on top of a motorcycle at nearly three miles a minute? The all-impressive thing is the colossal wind-pressure which tries to tear you backwards off the machine. Lift your head, and it is

MATCHLESS
MOTORCYCLES
1 9 3 5

MATCHLESS

George Brough (pictured here at Brooklands) was a decisive winner at the first attempt in 1922 on his side-valve, 976cc Brough Superior. Son of manufacturer W.E. Brough, George was a famous technician who built a number of one-off prototypes. Total production for the marque approached 3,000. In 1938 Fernihough's blown B-S was timed over the kilometre at 143.49mph, the highest speed attained at the Brooklands course by a two-wheeler.

Matchless, 1935. All Matchless 'racing' bikes of the inter-war period were modified sports models. During the thirties, engines were supplied to Brough Superior, OEG, Morgan, Coventry-Eagle, Calthorpe and their own AJS. In 1937 the Collier brothers bought Sunbeam, selling it on early in the war to the BSA group.

The Flying Featherweight: C.J.P. Dodson (right) at Brooklands in 1935 with speed king John Cobb (centre), an indelible hero at the track. Dodson was a member of the same Austin team as Pat Driscoll.

Norman Black at Mannin Beg, 1934. Mannin Moar and Mannin Beg (Great Man and Little Man in the Manx language) were races held in and around Douglas, on the Isle of Man. As a driver, Black campaigned MGs (Midget and Magnette), Maserati, Alfa Romeo and ERA.

forced back. If your goggles are not positioned very carefully, the lenses are pressed on to your eyeballs, and until you slow down you can't see a thing. Perhaps the most unexpected sensation is that of finding your cheeks flapping against your teeth like a rag in a breeze. The only way to avoid toothache is to suck in and hold them still.

The engine noise, after a certain speed, seems to fade away behind you, drowned in the roar of the wind. A narrow ribbon of concrete appears to be dashing towards and under you, edged by a blur of green, and the most welcome sight of all is the little group of timekeepers at the finish. You wonder if you can reach them without easing your speed; and then, having passed them, your concentration is absorbed in slowing, which must be done very gradually.

Danger? There must always be danger in exploring the unknown, and I was exploring speeds that had never been attained before on two wheels. But you don't think of it. There are so many other things to occupy your attention. I had one speed wobble – at

over 170 – and recovered in time to laugh at the spectators who were still trying to scramble over the roadside banks out of the way of the crash they imagined was coming. I nearly laughed myself into another. But one is enough – at that speed, at any rate.

Why do we do it? – what is the use of it? – people ask. Tourists travel now at the speeds I commenced racing at, though only 15 years have passed since then. My two-ton lorry is as fast as my first racing motorcycle. That is progress. Besides which, we do it for the sake of British prestige.

I wonder sometimes what that small boy who was once me would have thought of it all.

RACING BREEDS CAR CHAMPIONS
says Norman Ruck

Why do successful motor cyclists so often go to the top in the car racing game? There you have a question which offers endless scope for theorising and speculation.

Freddy Dixon's feats on two wheels go

back to pre-war days. In the early post-bellum T.T's his single-cylinder Indian with the backward-leaning cylinder had always to be reckoned with, even if it never won the senior race.

Later came the famous old 8-valve Harley-Davidson, so high and mulish that nobody but Freddy could have lapped Brooklands on it at the speed of which it was capable. At that period, or thereabouts, our Yorkshireman was busy making 600cc Douglases go faster that they'd ever gone before.

"FREDDY DIXON"

Next it was H.R.Ds and Brough Superiors. With the former, Freddy won the Junior T.T., walking busily up and down the footboards as he lapped. (Contrary to ordinary custom, Fred always used footboards in place of rests.) A special Brough, built to Dixon's pet ideas (and largely by Fred) sent the world's speed record rocketing up, and smashed the Brooklands sidecar lap record.

Then – exit from the bike game. New halls of fame were waiting and he rode into them in a Riley car, or rather a series of Rileys.

Freddy's record of subsequent racing successes is too long and too well known to recount in full. He is known and honoured in the car world as the man who makes an unsupercharged motor travel faster than most blown motors of similar size.

They call Freddy the tough guy. He hit a bank head-on at Donington with a force that would have pulped lesser men. The tough guy survived. At Montlhéry, driving Cobb's Napier-Railton on wet concrete, he held a skid that would have wrenched the arms out of you and I, thereby saving his own life and a few thousands' pounds worth of motor car. Then went flying, and the aeroplane "hit the deck" – hard.

He bought "Silver Bullet", the car which tried and failed to lower Sir Malcolm Campbell's speed record. After months of work he says it was stuff and nonsense they talked about the "Bullet" having a hoodoo, and being destined always for failure. But, he adds, these monster cars, which derive their speed purely from vast engine size, teach us nothing. So now he is to build something entirely different, something less than half "Bluebird's" size-and, he says, a lot faster!

We shall see, in good time, whether ex-motorcyclist Dixon can take motoring's richest prize from ex-motorcyclist Campbell.

And so to a second "D," Charlie Dodson. The light of C.J.P. Dodson, five feet and a few mm., first shone before men in the Amateur T.T. Then it was the T.T. itself and Charlie's rise to fame was sudden and spectacular. Always he was mounted on Sunbeams in the early part of his career, and Sunbeams had everybody else guessing at that period. Twice in succession he won the Senior T.T., riding with a polish which set one wondering whether after all there mightn't be such a thing as poetry in the motion of a motor cycle.

In the big Continental races, he piled victory on victory. Everywhere he went they said the same – his like had never been seen before, and as far as pure style went, would probably never be seen again.

Later, Charles did good things on Excelsiors. And later still four wheels claimed him. What then? Had his motorcycle experi-

Yorkshireman F.W. Dixon, 'Flying Freddy', gained a great reputation for toughness and mechanical ingenuity in motorcycling.

A beret-hatted L.P. Driscoll at Le Mans, 1932. Works driver for Austin, Pat Driscoll took British and International records at Brooklands. He was a prominent performer in the remarkably fast blown, side-valve Austin 7.

139

ence taught him anything that couldn't be learnt without the experience?

The answer, apparently, was – yes! Numerous lesser triumphs led up to a season both profitable and highly creditable in 1934. In the Douglas round-the-houses races he gave more than a hint of his true worth by finishing second in both the Mannin Beg and Mannin Moar races. Then came the real reward of driving skill, which by now was a long way above the average. He and M.G. Magnette won the Ulster T.T. itself, beating Hall's Bentley to the post in one of the finest finishes ever seen on the Ards circuit.

John Cobb paid Charlie the highest imaginable compliment by enlisting him to share with Rose-Richards and himself the task of gaining for Great Britain the big block of world's records held by Ab Jenkins; these including the coveted hour and 24 hours. So it came about that Dodson set off for the Bonneville Flats, Utah, on one of the greatest adventures in motoring annals. The sweeping triumphs of the Napier-Railton, to which C.J.P. contributed all of his share, is now a matter of history. What next, I wonder?

A third "D", Bert Denly – like Dodson, a man whose lowly stature contrasts with his gigantic strength – first got his chance in the early twenties, when he contrived to bring himself to the notice of D.R. O'Donovan, at the door of whose Brooklands shed Bert would frequently loiter, registering respectful awe.

The admiration was, so to speak, on the other foot after "Don" had given Denly a trying out on one of the miraculously fast side-

An outstandingly smart BMW R63, 1928. All BMWs built to 1929 – except the R39, which was discontinued – used the half-litre sv and ohc engine.
By the late thirties the grand prix scene saw technical progress reach the highest rate ever achieved. Supercharging produced some astounding results.

Chris Staniland in Dr. Roth's 105 Talbot at Brooklands, 1935. Staniland was an experienced test pilot and successful exponent of the JAP-engined racing Excelsior. He shared the wheel of the record-breaking 'Speed of the Wind' at Utah with George Eyston and Bert Denly.

Swiss Grand Prix, Berne 1951. The Berne circuit was situated on the western outskirts of the Swiss capital. A true road circuit, it was first used for motorcycle racing in 1931. The first car races were run in 1934 and it was the venue for Swiss Grands Prix before the government banned all racing in Switzerland in 1955. It was on this hazardous course, also known as Bremgarten, that the courageous Achille Varzi was killed in practice for the 1948 European GP. Truly, one of the golden figures from a golden age.

GRAND PRIX BERN

26./27. MAI 1951
CHAMPIONNATS DU MONDE

valve Nortons at the track. In those days, although speeds were naturally a long way below modern levels, it was no light matter to keep command of the tiller when things really got moving, for tyre sections were of pram calibre, shock absorbers unheard of and frames high without being mighty.

Denly, one might have imagined, would have found O'Donovan's models particularly unmanageable, for they boasted handle bars of a tortured curvature which brought the grips about on a level with the lower fork spindle, so that Bert, the slight of build, could scarcely reach the rubbers. But manage those Nortons he certainly did, and for season after season, at Brooklands and Montlhéry, he broke records, more records and yet more records.

In the later days, when Norton valves were no longer side by side, Denly had many a memorable scrap with Rex Judd and his Douglases, Bert le Vack and the J.A.Ps and New Hudsons, Vic Horsman (Triumphs) and A.G. Williams, that fine Sunbeam veteran.

After a term of service with R.M.N. Spring's A.J.S. équipe, Bert was seen no longer on motorcycles. Like Dixon and Dodson, he sought fresh fields to conquer, and those fields he ranged as the chosen jockey of George Eyston, the records specialist.

Cast your eye down the lists of international and world's records if you wish to know the deeds wrought by Denly. How many tens of thousands of miles has he covered on Montlhéry, I wonder? Records with Hotchkiss cars, records with Rileys, records with M.Gs, records with Delages. And last, but greatest of all, records with "Speed of the Wind", at Utah, sharing the wheel with Eyston and Chris Staniland, that other one-time motorcycle racer of widespread fame.

Light weight, compact build, extraordinary stamina and a cool head – these are the qualities which have taken Denly to the top of the tree in the record-breaking business. He was born light and compact, probably, but who is to say that his nerve and stamina were not founded on those spine-hammering rides of his earlier motorcycling days?

Then there is Pat Driscoll, our final "D". One remembers his Norton days more for his consistently good sidecar driving than for any outstanding flashes of brilliance, or for earth-shaking triumphs. A meeting seldom passed without Pat having a hand in the sport, and often enough in the spoils as well. I see him in my mind's eye hauling his trusty outfit round the sandbanks on the old motorcycle Grand Prix course, always with his heart right in the job and enjoying his sport as a sportsman should – for the sport's sake.

He ranks among the four most polished Brooklands Mountain Circuit and Shelsley drivers we have. Certainly the mad tunes he plays on his whining, howling Austin is one of the things which makes a race worth going to see. Until a few months ago, Driscoll held his class record for the Mountain course, and it was not many moons since he relinquished the International standing mile and kilometre records also. To appreciate what this means one must always bear in mind that the little brown "Seven" is a side-valve. Indeed it is said – and truthfully, I believe – that this car, with its 750cc engine, is the fastest s.v. car in the world, irrespective of size!

There are others, of course – dozens of them – Nuvolari, Varzi, Rosemeyer, Taruffi (designer-rider of the first 500cc machine to exceed 150mph), Ghersi, Black, Don, Handley, and numbers more.

You can, if you like, explain it by saying it just happened that way. Or, on the other hand, you may conclude simply that motorcycling is the finest training on earth for safe and fast car navigation. My vote is for the latter.

Acknowledgements

The publishers would like to express their gratitude to
the following individuals and organisations who have supplied
the illustrations in this book:

DUNLOP: 121;
BMW BILDARCHIV: 94, 95, 99 (upper), 125, 129,
134 (upper), 141 (upper);
NATIONAL MOTOR MUSEUM: 8, 11, 14, 17, 36, 42, 43, 48, 56, 58, 59, 60,
71 (lower), 75, 76, 77, 84, 88, 92 (lower), 98, 99 (lower), 100, 106,
108, 111, 112, 113, 114, 115, 116, 120, 122, 124, 128, 130, 131,
137, 140 (upper);
NATIONAL TECHNICAL MUSEUM (PRAGUE): 18, 31 (upper), 44.
ROBERT OPIE COLLECTION: 45, 46, 50, 82, 83, 126;
RAC: 25, 39, 49, 54, 55, 62, 63, 69;
MARY ANN ROBERTS: 2, 7, 13, 19, 20, 21, 22, 28, 30, 32, 33, 34, 40, 47
(upper), 52, 53, 57, 61, 64, 65, 66, 67, 70, 71 (upper), 72, 73, 74, 78
(lower), 80, 81, 85, 90, 91, 92 (middle), 93, 96, 97, 101, 102, 109, 110,
118, 119, 132, 134 (lower), 135, 136, 138, 139, 140 (lower), 141
(lower), 142.